THE LITERACY MAP

GUIDING CHILDREN TO WHERE THEY NEED TO BE

(K-3)

by

J. Richard Gentry

ACKNOWLEDGMENTS

The author and publisher wish to thank those who gave permission to reprint borrowed material. Every effort has been made to trace the ownership of all copyrighted materials in this book and to obtain permission for their use.

"Writing New Rules on Reading" by Tamara Henry. Copyright 1997, USA TODAY. Reprinted with permission.

"Keep Book" excerpt from *Guided Reading: Good First Teaching for All Children* by Irene C. Fountas and Gay Su Pinnell. Copyright © 1996 by Irene C. Fountas and Gay Su Pinnell. Heinemann, Portsmouth, NH.

"Making an Eight-Page Book" excerpt from *Invitations* by Regie Routman. © 1994. Heinemann, A division of Reed Elsevier Inc., Portsmouth, NH.

Excerpt from Stanovich, Keith E. (1993, December). "Romance and Reality". *The Reading Teacher*, 47(4), 280-291.

From *Pop Pops the Popcorn* by Bob Egan. © 1996 by Modern Curriculum Press. Used by permission.

Greedy Cat is Hungry by Joy Cowley. Illustrations by Robyn Belton.Text copyright © Joy Cowley 1987. Illustrations copyright © Crown 1987. Learning Media Limited, New Zealand 1997.

Amelia Bedelia by Peggy Parish. TEXT COPYRIGHT © 1963 BY MARGARET PARISH. PICTURES COPYRIGHT © 1963 BY FRITZ SIEBERT. Used by permission of HarperCollins Publishers. This selection may not be re-illustrated.

Frog and Toad Are Friends by Arnold Lobel. COPYRIGHT © 1970 BY ARNOLD LOBEL. Used by permission of HarperCollins Publishers. This selection may not be re-illustrated.

Bridges to Literacy. "Characteristics of Texts that Support Beginning Readers". © Barbara Peterson. The Ohio State University, 1988.

Excerpt from SHEEP IN A JEEP by Nancy Shaw and Margot Apple. Text copyright © 1986 by Nancy Shaw. Reprinted by permission of Houghton Mifflin Company. All rights reserved.

Goodnight Moon © Copyright 1947 BY HARPER & ROW, PUBLISHERS, INCORPORATED. TEXT COPYRIGHT RENEWED 1975 BY ROBERTA BROWN RAUCH. Used by permission of HarperCollins Publishers. This selection may not be re-illustrated.

Adapted by permission of Ellin Oliver Keene and Susan Zimmermann: MOSAIC OF THOUGHT: TEACHING COMPREHENSION IN A READER'S WORKSHOP (Heinemann, A division of Reed Elsevier Inc., Portsmouth, NH 1997).

Reprinted by permission of J. Richard Gentry: *My Kid Can't Spell: Understanding and Assisting Your Child's Literacy Development* (Heinemann, A division of Reed Elsevier Inc., Portsmouth, NH 1997).

From *Basic Reading Inventory: Preprimer Through Grade Twelve & Early Literacy Assessments*, Seventh Edition by Jerry L. Johns. Copyright © 1997 Kendall/Hunt Publishing Company. Used with permission.

An Observation Survey of Early Literacy Achievementt by Marie M. Clay. © 1993, Marie M. Clay. Heinemann.

The BFG by Roald Dahl. Illustrated by Quentin Blake. Text © Roald Dahl. Puffin Books.

Visit our web site at http://www.mondopub.com
Printed in Canada 00 01 02 03 04 05 06   9 8 7 6 5 4 3 2 1
Edited by Emmi S. Herman
Designed by Harry Chester, Inc.
Production by The Kids at Our House

Library of Congress Cataloging-in-Publication Data
Gentry, J. Richard.
    The literacy map : guiding children to where they need to be (K-3)/J. Richard Gentry.
      p.   cm.
Includes bibliographical references.
ISBN 1-572-55737-0 (pbk.)
      1. Language arts (Primary)—United States—Evaluation. 2.Literacy—United States.
      3. Educational tests and measurements—United States. I. Title.

LB1528.G45 1999
372.6 21—dc21   99-045900

CONTENTS

This book is dedicated to
Anyone who has ever taught someone else to read . . .
Those who inspire children to aspire literacy . . .
Those who inspire me—Bill, Bonnie, Stacy, Blake, and Bradsher

—J.R.G.

THIRTY-SEVEN QUESTIONS

What if you only had to ask 37 or fewer questions to determine whether a child met the minimum acceptable literacy criteria for your grade level? What if nearly half of those questions could be answered quickly and easily by looking at a child's writing and the remaining questions answered by observing a child in ordinary classroom activity? What if asking these questions enabled you to establish a map for each child's journey to literacy that would help you guide a child to where he or she needed to be? Would you be interested?

The 37 grade-level specific questions relate to 37 first-grade benchmarks that define first-grade literacy success. (There are 28 kindergarten benchmarks, 34 second-grade benchmarks, and 40 third-grade benchmarks.) The answers will enable you to guide children to exactly where they need to be for success at the next grade level. The benchmarks override teaching philosophy, pedagogy, and the particular reading program you may be using. They are mileposts on each child's personal journey to literacy, marking achievement in essential areas of balanced literacy instruction. The benchmarks in this book provide the map you need to guide each child in your classroom to literacy success.

This book grew out of my work with teachers, school districts, and state departments of education across the country that are moving to higher standards, accountability, and balanced literacy instruction. It is based on research and experience—27 years as a teacher, reading center director, professor, author, and educational consultant for teachers of literacy in the classroom. It draws from my teaching career helping to guide hundreds of children to learn to read, write, and spell and from my observing what works in successful classrooms around the country.

Most likely you already know a lot about the teaching of literacy. This book will extend your knowledge and help you tie the essential elements of literacy instruction at your grade level into even more successful balanced literacy instruction.

J. Richard Gentry, Ph.D.

CHAPTER 1

YOU NEED A MAP

Soon after moving to Chicago I purchased a city map. Getting around Carl Sandburg's "stormy, husky, brawling, city of big shoulders" can be complex and intimidating. I needed a reliable map to help me get where I wanted to go.

Similarly, at the beginning of each school year, when new students enter your classroom, you are venturing into unfamiliar territory, and you need a map—a literacy map. This map can help you know if your students' reading, writing, and spelling is appropriate for their age. Using the literacy map, you can accurately assess students' literacy competencies, then chart their literacy course for the school year. Without a literacy map, you'll find yourself—and your students—floundering. Once you know your grade level territory thoroughly, you may not need the map as often, but if teaching new students has as many twists, turns, and unexpected detours as Chicago, you'll find yourself pulling out the map again and again.

The literacy map provides expected learning outcomes or benchmarks for the end of each grade. *Benchmarks are minimum acceptable literacy criteria for what should be happening during the year for each student in your classroom.* As essential aspects of each child's literacy develops, benchmarks help you track the progress.

Since schools are organized in grade levels, it makes sense to use a map with grade level benchmarks. We need grade level benchmarks that have developmental integrity, but these benchmarks should be based on the fact that chronological age or grade level provides fairly accurate criteria for what should be happening with literacy development. Time and time again, I have seen teachers go astray, because they didn't know the expected literacy learning outcomes for their grade level. These teachers had no map to guide them.

DO YOU KNOW WHERE YOU'RE GOING?
(Why You Need a Map and How to Use It)

Depending on grade level, as many as eleven essential literacy elements may be developing at the same time. The literacy map must represent layers of various aspects of reading, writing, and spelling developing synergisticly.

Beginning on page 129, you'll find a complete map outlining students' literacy growth at your grade level. This representation is not the journey itself any more than a map of Chicago is Chicago. The map is certainly not your curriculum. You are not scripted in any way. You must make many important curricula decisions to support the literacy journey.

Whatever your teaching philosophy, there are certain desired learning outcomes expected in every K-3 classroom. You will find these represented on the literacy map and be able to filter them through your own philosophy, values, and teaching experience. This map will not limit you in any way or dictate how you teach. Rather, its learning benchmarks will provide the structure you need to assess, plan, and teach effectively. It will help you guide your students where you want them to go and enable you to decide whether you have succeeded.

Let's start with a mini-map to give you an idea of how a literacy map can help us understand what should be happening and where we are going. We'll begin by limiting our view to spelling development in kindergarten and first grade. Because the purpose here is to help you frame a mental picture of how a literacy map works, this information about spelling will be covered again in the appropriate grade level literacy map.

A MINI-LITERACY MAP OF SPELLING
FOR KINDERGARTEN AND FIRST GRADE

On the journey to spelling competence, children should:

Kindergarten
- Develop an ear for sounds in words
- Develop an ear for rhymes
- Begin to demonstrate phonemic awareness (i.e., awareness of some phonemes in initial, medial, and final intraword positions)
- Demonstrate knowledge of the alphabet
- Recognize that letters represent sounds
- Split syllables into sounds
- Match letters with phonemes in words
- Invent Stage 1 spellings (first half of year)
- Invent Stage 2 spellings (end of year)

> *First Grade*
>
> - Demonstrate full phonemic awareness (middle of year)
> - Invent Stage 3 spellings (middle of year)
> - Invent Stage 4 spellings (end of year)
> - Begin to develop consciousness for correct spelling of first-grade-level words
> - Spell some high frequency word families correctly (end of year)
> - Spell some high frequency words correctly (e.g., *the, of, have, go*)
> - Spell high frequency short vowel patterns correctly (end of year)
> - Spell many high frequency long vowel patterns correctly, such as *make, like* (end of year)

As this mini-map shows, spelling begins in kindergarten with the understanding that words are composed of speech sounds. Kindergarten children develop an ear for sounds in words and an ear for rhymes. Working with sounds during the kindergarten year should enable children to become "phonemically aware" and to differentiate specific sounds (phonemes) in initial, medial, and final positions. This work is preparation for the time in first grade when they can identify all the sounds in a one-syllable word like *bake* (/b/ +/ay/+/k/) or *cat* (/k/+/a/+/t/). They are then prepared to do activities like these:

1. Identify the two sounds in *no*. (/n/+/o/)
2. Blend phonemes such as /n/, /i/, /s/ into a word. (nice)
3. Say a word like *same* and delete a phoneme.
   ("Say *same* without the /m/." say)

Notice this "spelling work" is oral. It has nothing to do with letters of the alphabet.

At the same time, kindergarten children should be learning the letters of the alphabet, and by the end of the year, should know many letters. They should be able to name the letters, recognize them, write them, and show that they know something about the sounds the letters commonly represent. This is part of what kindergarten children must do to learn how spelling works. Taken together, sounds and recognition of letters lead kindergarten children to a point where they can match letters with phonemes in words to demonstrate that they know something about how sounds and symbols relate. These writing and spelling activities—understanding words are made of sounds, phonemic awareness, knowledge of the alphabet, matching letters with phonemes in words, understanding sound and symbol relationships—are major kindergarten year benchmarks that should be standard in every kindergarten classroom. As we shall see later, knowledge about the alphabet and its sounds is causally related to learning to read and should be considered a necessary foundation for most children to experience success in first grade.

The spelling mini-map shows us that all kindergarten children should be encouraged to use invented spellings. Not only does using invented spelling help children develop as writers and spellers, invented spelling is directly connected to success with beginning reading. While we've purposely limited our discussion in chapter one to a mini-map in spelling development, take note that kindergarten spelling and beginning reading are closely linked. It's well known that some children write first in invented spelling and read later (Chomsky, 1979). More specifically, research demonstrates that a first grader's invented spelling can have positive effects on his or her word recognition (Clarke, 1988). This isn't surprising since the only two kinds of knowledge known to be causally related to learning to read—knowledge of the alphabet and phonemic awareness—are the same kinds of knowledge learned, used, practiced, and extended when kindergartners and first graders invent spellings. Studies show word recognition takes on more importance in kindergarten and first grade, because the beginning reader's comprehension is, to some degree, "word recognition bound" (Juel, 1994). In other words, the more words beginning readers recognize, the better they read and comprehend. Invented spelling certainly ties into this fact: according to a study by Ehri and Wilce, spelling ability fosters word recognition by enabling a letter-sound association storage of words in memory (1987). The relationship between knowledge of the alphabet and phonemic awareness to invented spelling, then, links invented spelling in kindergarten and first grade very closely to word recognition, and word recognition is a linchpin to reading success. Richgels's empirical study found inventive spellers to be especially prepared for the use of phonetic knowledge that beginning reading requires (1995). While literacy knowledge must develop in numerous areas, invented spelling has been clearly shown to be important for beginning readers.

Invented spelling goes into reading like a key ingredient goes into a cake. 1) Mix phonemic awareness with knowledge of the alphabet. 2) Pour the resulting batter of authentic writing into a bowl whipped up by invented spelling. 3) Add phonics instruction. 4) Stir until word recognition is evident. 5) Bake in an environment of exposure to books that brings out meaning and the functions of written language. 6) Serve with authentic purpose. Enjoy!

Let's take a closer look at the mini-map of K-1 spelling to see how it can help us avoid the pitfalls of traveling without a map. It's normal for kindergarten children to begin the year inventing spellings without realizing that letters represent sounds. By year's end, however, kindergartners following the literacy map should be independently producing spellings that match letters with some of the phonemes in words. Children's initial attempts at using random letters to label drawings or write messages evolve into spelling such as KT for *cat* and BDA for *birthday*. Here's how it looks:

STAGE 1, "THE BABBLING LEVEL OF SPELLING"
(The Precommunicative Stage)
A benchmark for the first half of kindergarten

A grocery list by a Stage 1 speller:

EGOS (branflakes)
FISOS (milk)
MSOOE (doughnuts)

Note that you cannot read Stage 1 spelling.

Early in the kindergarten year, children should draw, label, and attempt to write for a purpose. Scribbling leads to the production of letter forms to represent labels or messages. Children should be doing this kind of temporary spelling in the first half of kindergarten as their level of alphabet knowledge grows from repetition of a few known letters to substantial production of many different letters. The literacy map indicates that we can expect to see a change in invented spelling by the end of the kindergarten year. Children are expected to move to Stage 2 as they conceptualize that letters represent sounds and that they can use the letters to spell the sounds they hear in words.

STAGE 2, "ABBREVIATED SPELLING"
(The Semiphonetic Stage)
A benchmark for the end of kindergarten

The literacy map shows that by the end of kindergarten, children should be matching letters to sounds and using those letters to represent words, even though these representations may be partial or abbreviated (e.g., BDA for *birthday* or E for *eagle*) or mixed with random letters (e.g., BSPHN for *baseball*). These conditions make end-of-kindergarten-year Stage 2 spellings hard to read without context or picture clues. Can you read these Stage 2 spellings?

IDS CWLS LEFT RSDHF

Here are the words: *ideas, quilts, elephant,* and *rainbow.*

STAGE 3, "SPELLING BY EAR"
(The Phonetic Stage)
A benchmark for middle of first grade

According to the literacy map, Stage 3 spellings should appear in the middle of first grade. Contrast these Stage 3 spellings with the Stage 2 spellings above.

wn nit I wus n mi
Bad and the tuth
Fare cam.

DER A M E
PLES
TO mi coM
PRT

There is quite a difference!

While first-grade teachers continue to encourage a great deal of invented spelling, they have different expectations than kindergarten teachers. By midyear of first grade, children should be moving into a level of spelling at which they can use letters to represent all the sounds in words. For the first time, they are able to provide a total mapping of letter-sound correspondence. They systematically develop predictable spellings for certain details of phonetic form: tense vowels, lax vowels, preconsonantal nasals, syllabic sonorants, *-ed* endings, retroflex vowels, affricates, and intervocalic flaps (Gentry 1978; Read 1975). By the middle of first grade, children should be able to write anything they can say, and though it may not look like English spelling, almost anyone can read it.

This mini-map specifies changes that should be happening with invented spelling by the middle of first grade. And in a successful first-grade classroom, encouraging invented spelling is balanced with modeled, shared, and interactive writing as well as plenty of spelling instruction. Between August and January, first graders should be learning to spell many words correctly. The first-grade teacher is paying attention to what each child knows and has a pretty good idea of how the child's spelling is progressing.

By the end of first grade the mini-map shows us that first graders should spell correctly some high frequency word families (e.g., *-at* in *at, cat, fat, rat*) and some high frequency short vowel patterns. In addition, they should spell correctly some high frequency long vowel patterns such as the final *e* marker pattern in *take* and *like* and they should demonstrate correct spelling of many high frequency words with irregular spellings such as *have, was, love, of.*

The complete literacy map shows that invented spelling should be in balance with spelling instruction. The literacy map eliminates the view that children's literacy development just happens.

Here's one instance when a teacher needed a map for kindergarten and first-grade spelling.

In September of 1997, I spoke at an event called "Parent University" in Pasadena Independent School District, a large suburb of Houston. Presenters were sharing information on various topics of interest to parents—adolescent nutrition, Internet access, HIV, gangs, dyslexia. I conducted a session called "Spelling and Literacy." At one point in the presentation, a mother in the back of the audience waved her hand frantically.

"Can you help me?" she asked. "My son *hates* spelling!"

"I'll try," I responded. "Tell me about him."

"Well, he's in first grade and he's really struggling with his spelling words."

The mother's account of the situation didn't make sense to me. You can see from the literacy map what's supposed to happen with spelling in first grade. Children aren't supposed to be struggling to memorize a lot of spelling words in September. They might be learning word families or regular phonics patterns, but it would not make sense that in September a first grader was "failing spelling." I would have understood the situation had the mother reported her son did not know any letters of the alphabet or could not read any words. Her son's consternation over "spelling" had already built up to "hate."

As we have seen on the literacy map, in September of first grade, children should be making a transition into a level of invented spelling at which they spell all the sounds they hear in words. It's expected that children may be inventing temporary spellings such as BAK for *bake,* SISTR for *sister,* and EGL for *eagle.* The map also shows what should be happening instructionally: A first grader who is developmentally on track might be learning high frequency regular phonics patterns and perhaps internalizing automatic spellings of some phonograms such as the *-at* spelling pattern in *cat, bat, rat, sat,* and *fat.* This kind of activity is so basic that one would expect such instruction in every first-grade classroom, regardless of the teacher's philosophy or the reading materials being used. Nothing should be happening in September, however, to make a child "hate spelling." Completely baffled, I asked the mother why she thought her son hated spelling.

"Well, he's struggling with his spelling words! This week he had *brother* and *through*. He just can't seem to learn them!"

What's shocking about this story is that a child and a mother are really suffering because his teacher is apparently oblivious to what should be happening in September of the first-grade year. If this parent reported what was happening accurately, it's reasonable to assume the teaching in her son's classroom was developmentally inappropriate. *Bat* might be a good spelling word for late September of first grade, but the appropriateness of *brother* and *through* is questionable. *Brother* should be mastered in second or third grade, and *through* in third, fourth, or fifth. Many first graders can't even read *brother* and *through* in September, much less spell them!

You may think this is an isolated incident, but I assure you it is not. Everywhere I have worked I encounter teachers who ask for a useful literacy map. "This is a need," they say, "why don't you fill it?" *The Literacy Map: Guiding Children to Where They Need to Be (K-3)* fills the void. If you teach K-3, you need to know the expected learning outcomes for your particular grade level and the end-of-year benchmarks that will prepare your students for success at the next grade level. Without a literacy map of expected learning outcomes, you can't assess, plan, or teach effectively.

In Chapter 1 we have explored the idea that you need a literacy map and that mapping out spelling development is relatively concrete. Since you can "see" spelling, you can use it to "see" other important aspects of a child's literacy development. In Chapter 2 we will use the map to see how observing spelling and writing allows you to assess many important early literacy benchmarks and how the map helps you know what to check. Before leaving "You Need a Map," however, here's a list of ways a literacy map might be used.

WAYS A LITERACY MAP CAN HELP YOU

Assessing children's literacy competencies
Knowing each child individually
Measuring each child's growth or progress
Planning effectively
Knowing what to teach
Knowing which literacy benchmarks to expect
    when using integrated curricula
Being accountable to parents/caregivers
Evaluating the effectiveness of your teaching

CHAPTER 2

KNOW YOUR STUDENTS INDIVIDUALLY

Each year when you enter your classroom, you have two literacy challenges. First, you must know the literacy map—the desired learning outcomes of your particular grade level. This knowledge will enable you to assess, plan, and teach effectively. Second, you must work quickly to know individually all the students in your classroom. You can start by asking these questions:

> Is this child reading independently?
> On what level is this child reading?
> What kind(s) of books will be just right for this child?
> What are her attitudes about books?
> How is this child coming along as a writer?
> What is she passionate about and how can I cultivate her passion into reading and writing?
> What words and patterns can this child spell?
> What important spelling work does this child need?

Every teacher must answer these questions about each student.

When you know both the literacy map and your students, you can use that information to guide your students' literacy learning while they are in your classroom. Something as simple as a child's writing sample can become a powerful tool for assessment. Here is a writing sample produced by a girl in November of her first-grade year.

The Three Little Pigs

One day a mother pig sent her three little pigs out into the woods. The first little pig met a man with a bundle of straw. The pig said to the man, "Give me straw to build my house."

Now read the story again in the child's original spelling.

> The three **PIG'S** Lillte
> one bay a Muthr
> PIG Sent.
> her three Lillte
> PIG'S Ot inot
> The WOD'S
> The Frst Litl PiG
> Met a MaN With
> a BuN DL U V.
> CtR o The PiG SeD
> tA te MaN GiV ME
> CtoR tO BilD my huose

Let's look at this child as a speller and a writer and ask a simple question: What does she know? We will use this one sample to place the child on the literacy map by checking off literacy map benchmarks at important checkpoints. Limiting our view of this child to *one writing sample at one point in time* illustrates the power of knowing the map and knowing this child individually.

Because I know the literacy map, I am familiar with the territory this young child is navigating. She is in first grade, a critical time in the literacy journey for most children. This is the year she should become an independent reader, and that should be her first-grade teacher's ultimate goal. *Reading is the most important accomplishment in the basic education of a child.* The literacy map directs me to two questions I can ask that will predict whether she is likely to be successful with reading in first grade:

1) Does she have knowledge of the alphabet?
2) Does she have phonemic awareness?

Although work towards achieving alphabet knowledge and phonemic awareness begins in kindergarten, the first-grade teacher should ask these two critical questions about each student at the beginning of first grade. It's well documented that reaching alphabet and phonemic awareness benchmarks are necessary though not sufficient for success with reading, and their importance resides in the fact that they are the only factors known to be causally related to first-grade reading achievement (Stanovich, 1994). If the girl knows the alphabet and has phonemic awareness, I can predict she will be successful with reading in first grade. Does the November writing sample confirm that these two necessary but not sufficient conditions for her success as a first-grade reader are present? Let's look at the sample to find out.

Does she have knowledge of the alphabet? The answer is *yes*. Substantive alphabet knowledge is required for a child to produce a writing sample at this level of sophistication.

Does she have phonemic awareness? Again the answer is *yes*. Spellings such as MUTHR, LITL, GIV, BILD, SED, and WOD'S demonstrate she has full phonemic awareness. Not only is she able to segment all the speech sounds in these words, she can go a step further and match the sounds with letters to create readable spelling.

With these two observations alone, the writing sample predicts this child is well on her way to learning to read in first grade, given an appropriate environment, focused instruction, and exposure to books. When the teacher knows precisely what to look for, it is possible that something as elemental as a writing sample can yield powerful information.

The literacy map provides at least 24 other kindergarten and first-grade benchmark checkpoints relevant to our young writer's literacy development. Let's look at them and then use the questions to sift through the information that is abundant in this writing sample. By asking the right questions, we can know this writer individually.

BENCHMARK QUESTIONS ADDRESSED IN THE SAMPLE

Kindergarten

- Does she have the concept of word?
- Can she make the voice to print match?
- Does she understand that words are composed of speech sounds?
- Can she identify the sounds in a one-syllable word?
- Does she recognize and name all uppercase and lowercase letters?
- Does she understand the alphabet principle?
- Can she associate sounds with the letters of the alphabet?
- Can she recognize some words by sight?
- Can she spell some words automatically?
- Can she listen and comprehend stories read aloud?
- Can she retell stories or parts of stories?
- Does she independently write most uppercase and lowercase letters?

First Grade

- Can she count or clap the number of syllables in a word?
- Does she demonstrate full phonemic awareness?
- Can she accurately decode phonetically regular, one-syllable words and nonsense words?
- Can she spell a collection of first-grade-level spelling words correctly?
- Has she moved into Stage 3 (Phonetic spelling)—"spelling by ear" and representing virtually all the sounds in words?
- Has she moved beyond Stage 3 to Stage 4 (Transitional spelling)—representing many of the visual aspects of English spelling?
- Does she spell three and four-letter, short-vowel words correctly?
- Does she spell some high frequency irregular sight words correctly?
- Can she produce a variety of types of short compositions?
- Does she use basic punctuation and capitalization?
- Does she express ideas, think creatively, and organize information in ways that are appropriate for her grade level?
- Does she demonstrate age appropriate world knowledge?

Judging from the writing sample, our young writer has met all the benchmarks listed above. Her sample shows evidence of concept of word and voice to print match—benchmarks typically assessed through reading activity but certainly inherent in a child's writing.

Her full phonemic awareness eliminates any concern one might have regarding subordinate knowledge about speech sounds. She knows words are made of speech sounds and she can identify speech sounds in a one-syllable word. Based on her successful phonetic spelling of the two-syllable words—BUNDL, LITL, and MUTHR—one can assume she can count their syllables.

Spelling entails both knowledge of the alphabet and phonemic awareness, and this writer's sample illustrates her full control of both predictors. She handles the alphabet skillfully, indicating that she can recognize and independently write the uppercase and lowercase letters. She uses uppercase and lowercase letters indiscriminately, however, and a good observer would make note to teach her the basic rules for capitalization.

One could also extrapolate from her spelling that she associates sounds with the letters of the alphabet and fully understands the alphabet principle. How else would she spell words so we can read them? It's a good bet she spells a few words automatically, a bet easily confirmed with a test or further observation of her spelling in writing. I would guess *one, pig, her, with, a, me,* and *my* are in her automatic spelling vocabulary though she wavers on *the* and reverses *d* to *b* in *day.* Her teacher might note the reversal, watch out for it in future writing, and work on correcting it if it's a problem.

This particular instance of real writing in the classroom—a child's choice to produce her own version of the Joseph Jacobs' rendition of a story she had heard read in class—provides a concrete opportunity to observe her ability to listen, comprehend, and retell stories or parts of stories. The writing sample verifies these benchmarks are coming along nicely.

Not only does placing this child on the literacy map tell us where she is now, it informs our future instruction. For example, it would make sense to monitor the child's development of phonics knowledge and continue phonics instruction and appropriate first grade spelling instruction in her curriculum. She handles some regular c-v-c words—*pig, met, man*—and puts phonics knowledge to use when writing GIV for the irregular phonics pattern *give,* SED for *said,* BILD for *build,* UV for *of,* BUN for the first syllable of *bundle,* and MUTH for the first syllable of *mother.* However, she is limited and neither confident nor consistent in her use of phonics. Much more writing, phonics, and spelling work is needed before she becomes comfortable with alternative spelling patterns or develops a high degree of word specific knowledge. She certainly needs to learn the correct spelling of *the, of,* and *to* because she will use these phonic irregular words almost every time she writes. While this first grader spells nine first-grade-level words correctly in this piece—*one, a, pig, sent, her, met, with, me, my*—forty-four percent of the words in her story are misspelled. One goal before the end of first grade will be to increase her collection of known first-grade-level spelling words.

Another major goal should be learning to use basic punctuation and capitalization. She's not clear on when to use uppercase and lowercase letters, periods, or apostrophes. Much more experience with reading and writing in the coming months should further develop her ability to express ideas, organize information, think creatively, and expand her knowledge of the world.

It is relevant to do a developmental spelling analysis and ask if our young writer has moved beyond Stage 3 spelling to Stage 4.

DEVELOPMENTAL ANALYSIS OF INVENTED SPELLING IN *THE THREE LITTLE PIGS*

Misspelling	Word	Developmental Stage	
TA	to	Semiphonetic	Stage 2
TE	the	Semiphonetic	Stage 2
UV	of	Phonetic	Stage 3

Misspelling	Word	Developmental Stage	
SED	said	Phonetic	Stage 3
OT	out	Phonetic	Stage 3
LITL	little	Phonetic	Stage 3
MUTHR	mother	Phonetic	Stage 3
FRST	first	Phonetic	Stage 3
GIV	give	Phonetic	Stage 3
WOD'S	woods	Phonetic	Stage 3
BUNDL	bundle	Phonetic	Stage 3
CTRO	straw	Phonetic	Stage 3
CTOR	straw	Phonetic	Stage 3
BILD	build	Phonetic	Stage 3
HUOSE	house	Transitional	Stage 4
LILLTE	little	Transitional	Stage 4
PIG'S	pigs	Transitional	Stage 4
BAY	day	(letter reversal)	
INOT	into	Transitional	Stage 4

11% Semiphonetic (Stage 2)
67% Phonetic (Stage 3)
22% Transitional (Stage 4)

This analysis shows that this writer is a phonetic speller (Stage 3) moving into transitional spelling (Stage 4). According to our literacy map, she is a little ahead of where we would expect her to be. She already meets the midyear Stage 3 spelling benchmark in November. She is not yet a Stage 4 speller and often doesn't use the visual conventions of English spelling. Our expectation from the literacy map is that she will move from the November strategy of spelling primarily by ear to a more sophisticated Stage 4 strategy, including the visual patterns of English, spelling by the end of the year. (For information on how to analyze developmental spelling see Gentry, J. R. *My Kid Can't Spell!* Portsmouth, NH: Heinemann (1997); see also Gentry, J. R. and Gillet, J. *Teaching Kids To Spell*. Portsmouth, NH: Heinemann (1993).)

A word frequency analysis also reveals information to help us know this child individually and place her on the literacy map. While her spelling is quite good for November of the first-grade year, she has not learned to correctly spell many of the words she will be using most frequently in her writing. The chart on the next page uses Smith and Ingersoll's *Written Vocabulary of Elementary School Pupils: Ages 4-6* (1984) to see how frequently each word she misspelled in *The Three Little Pigs* story might generally be used in children's writing.

WORD FREQUENCY ANALYSIS OF INVENTED SPELLING
IN *THE THREE LITTLE PIGS*

Misspelling	Word	Most Frequently Used Words
UV	of	Among top 10
TA	to	Among top 10
TE	the	Among top 10
SED	said	Among top 40
OT	out	Among top 60
BAY	day	Among top 60
HUOSE	house	Among top 80
LILLTE	little	Among top 100
LITL	little	Among top 100
MUTHR	mother	Among top 110
INOT	into	Among top 110
FRST	first	Among top 120
GIV	give	Among top 140
PIG'S	pigs	Not in the top 500
WOD'S	woods	Not in the top 500
BUNDL	bundle	Not in the top 500
CTRO	straw	Not in the top 500
CTOR	straw	Not in the top 500
BILD	build	Not in the top 500

Thirteen of the 19 misspelled words are among the 500 words children use most in their writing. It can be expected that the writer will use many of these same words again and again when she writes. These words, then, would be appropiate words to teach as spelling words, especially words such as *of, to,* and *the* which are among the ten words children use most often when writing. We know she does not know how to spell these words, so we'll teach them. That's how the literacy map and knowing children individually works.

Do you think we have now squeezed *The Three Little Pigs* story for all it's worth? It seems incredible that so much information about one child's literacy development can be found in a one-page story. We were able to keep squeezing and squeezing, because we had a literacy map to help us know which questions to ask. We went a long way in placing the little girl on the literacy map—and a long way in knowing her individually.

Up to this point, we have limited our view of the literacy map. Chapter 1 focused on a K-1 literacy map for spelling and Chapter 2 on relevant benchmarks in a single piece of writing. Now, let's expand our view.

A complex literacy map must show layers of information and represent all essential requirements for literacy development at a particular grade level. At the same time an effective map must be concrete and specific. The benchmarks on the map must be specific to each grade level.

A map for first grade might show the following ten elements of literacy developing simultaneously: listening comprehension, exposure to print, reading comprehension and fluency, phonemic awareness, knowledge of regular phonics patterns, word specific knowledge, writing development, spelling development, ideas and world knowledge, and attitudes about reading and writing. Not only may these be developing at the same time, but the development of one affects the development of another. For example, an increase in a first grader's spelling sophistication leads to better sight word recognition, and this expands the child's reading comprehension. As we shall see in the following chapters, all the elements are important for a particular child's development.

To know a particular student, a teacher must look through all ten layers of information cited above. This is easy to do because the benchmarks in these ten essential elements of literacy are clearly specified and the benchmarks provide a map of concrete things to look for in each child's development. It's also easy because you might be observing reading comprehension and see phonics development, or while you're observing the child's writing, you can clearly see spelling development. As we saw with *The Three Little Pigs* writing sample, a lot of the information necessary to pinpoint the child's position on the map is right in front of us—even in a single writing sample.

The chapters that follow provide a map of specific and concrete benchmarks to make it much easier for you to meet the challenge of knowing your students individually. You will not only find information on assessment, but teaching activities as well. Before we get to assessment and teaching activities, however, we must consider your schedule and the importance of time—time to read, write, and spell.

CHAPTER 3

IT'S ABOUT TIME!
(CREATE A SCHEDULE THAT WORKS)

Regardless of what pedagogy you follow, how children spend their time in your classroom is critical for their literacy development. You can't consider all the essential elements on the literacy map without thinking about how children are spending their time. I often observe teachers achieving success with various teaching techniques, but their success is almost always a result of the time their students spend reading, writing, spelling, and learning about words. It's imperative that educators pay more attention to how students spend their time.

You know the old saying, "Three things determine the value of a piece of real estate: location, location, location." I believe three things determine the successful development of literacy: time, time, time. Stand in the doorway of your classroom and ask yourself these questions: "How are my students spending their time? Are they reading independently and receiving small group instruction? Are they receiving focused instruction and spending time writing? Do children in my classroom spend an appropriate amount of time with spelling—finding words, inspecting words, mastering words, and developing better spelling habits?" Not only must children in your classroom have access to books that are just right for them, they must spend time engaged with these books. Success comes when children spend time reading, writing, spelling, learning vocabulary, creating ideas, and expanding their knowledge. If you see children engaged in these literacy acts, they are learning and their literacy is growing. Nothing is more important than how the children in your classroom spend their time.

Time is of the essence in the teaching of literacy. Too often we miss that fact. A Section D cover story in *USA Today* on January 29, 1997, titled "Writing New Rules on Reading," is a powerful commentary on how time spent reading often leads to success even though gimmickry and gadgetry is often touted as the cause for reading gains. Here's the story.

WRITING NEW RULES ON READING
The push is on to ensure literacy by third grade
By Tamara Henry and Beth Ashley, USA TODAY

Two years ago, Vicky Velasquez was a fourth-grader who couldn't read.

Frustrated with constant schoolwork failures, Vicky had become a withdrawn 10-year-old. That was before Diane Crawford, principal at Robb Elementary School in Uvalde, Texas, tested Vicky and found she was an "extremely kinetic learner"—that is, she learned best through motion.

The solution: The youngster was taught pep squad cheers that gave each letter of the alphabet a body movement.

"Somehow or another it clicked in her mind," Crawford says. "So when taking spelling tests, she pictures herself outside, making the moves."

Vicky is now a "solid" sixth-grader. The strategy, though unconventional, was successful. And that's what matters to Crawford. When it comes to reading she says, "We really work with the child until we find something that works."

When I read this, I nearly fell out of my chair. Here's *USA TODAY* reporting the secret to teaching reading as being pep squad cheers! Vicky may indeed have grown into a "'solid' sixth-grader," but it was her muscles and not her reading skill that had been pumped up by pep squad cheers! I kept reading.

The ability to read is a fundamental skill. Yet nearly half of the 44 million Kindergarten-12th grade public school children can't read well. The nation's Reading Report Card showed that in 1994, 41% of fourth-graders were reading below grade level, as were 31% of eighth-graders and 25% of high school seniors.

What caused Vicky Velasquez to become a better reader? Seven columns later on the back page of the article, I found the answer. Vicky had been in a special reading program for several years. The assistant superintendent offered this explanation for why reading test scores had risen:

...you have to be very focused on reading and very committed. ... That means that we sometimes teach reading more than once during the day. We sometimes keep the kids after school and work on reading. We work with them in the summer on reading.

Did pep squad cheers cause Vicky Velasquez to become a better reader? I don't think so. It was time—time spent with good reading instruction, along with time spent reading.

I have the opportunity to visit classrooms across the country. I visit some of the best schools and some of the worst schools in America, and when I walk into a school where success is achieved in the teaching of reading and writing, there's one common element. In every instance, I see children reading and writing.

Here's an activity to help you consider whether your kindergarten classroom is a reading/writing classroom: First think of one child in your classroom. Visualize the child's name in this blank: _____. Now you are ready for the exercise.

There are about seven hours, or 420 minutes, in a school day. Imagine you are a researcher. Your study requires you to determine how children spend their time in school. You will observe one child. You arrive at the child's school before the school day begins. You have a clipboard with 420 slots on a spreadsheet—one slot for each minute of the school day. Your task is to write down what this child is doing at the beginning of each minute of the school day. When the 420 slots are filled in at the end of the day, how many minutes did you observe the child reading? How many minutes writing?

My experience of observing successful reading/writing classrooms is that a reading/writing classroom is one in which children are reading independently for about 45 minutes of the school day; they are writing independently for about 45 minutes. When I say "the child is reading," I mean reading literally—not sitting in a whole class reading group waiting for a turn to perform (which would be noted on your clipboard as "waiting"). Reading/writing classrooms are places where children read and write independently in addition to receiving a lot of small group instruction.

If you are thinking that your students have so many "pull-out" activities, they can't possibly receive instruction and read and write independently every day, then you have discovered a problem: Children shouldn't be pulled out during times when they should be reading and writing. Since you are held responsible for the literacy development of the children in your classroom, you want the time to teach them. Their time must be carefully guarded. Children need to spend time focused on reading, writing, and spelling to fully develop literacy in each of these areas. You can't be successful with individuals who are continually pulled out of your classroom.

When you consider that there are 420 minutes in an entire school day, 45 minutes of independent reading and 45 minutes of independent writing over the course of the day sound like reasonable goals. Why "45 minutes"? It is what I see recommended by researchers and teacher researchers (Atwell, 1998; Calkins, 1991; Graves, 1983, 1994; Routman, 1991,1997), what I see happening in classrooms where children are successfully developing in literacy, and what I believe makes good sense. If our goal is excellent basic education and literacy development, children should spend their time in school reading, writing, and spelling.

Many schedules can accommodate your goal of creating a classroom where children read, write, spell, and receive instructional guidance. Let's look at a schedule for kindergarten through grade three and some basic teaching practices in successful reading/writing classrooms. Children following this schedule will spend a lot of time reading and writing in school and are much more likely to meet the middle-and-end-of-year-benchmarks outlined on the literacy map.

The reading workshop runs for one hour and may be divided into three segments: independent reading (20 minutes), shared reading (20 minutes), and guided reading (20 minutes). Each segment combines a number of teaching strategies that vary at different instructional levels. Here's what happens in each segment of the schedule. In independent reading, the children are reading independently while the teacher is conferencing with individuals or working with small guided reading groups. In shared reading, the teacher teaches skills and strategies to the whole class. In guided reading, the teacher meets with small guided reading groups while children not participating in the groups are reading independently or participating in literacy centers.

The schedule becomes a routine and *creates an expectation:* "Settle down, children," it says. "For the next hour, we'll all be reading." I like it when I walk into a classroom and reading is the expectation—reading is the business of first through third-grade classrooms.

The sections that follow provide snapshots of some of the procedures you might observe in a successful reading workshop.

DAILY READING WORKSHOP

INDEPENDENT READING   20 MINUTES

During the first twenty minutes of a reading workshop, everyone is reading independently. In a first-grade classroom, you might observe children with book bags. The teacher has matched each child with books that are just right for the child. (See Matching Children With Books on page 75.) You might notice color-coded tubs or bins filled with leveled texts or the classroom might be operating out of a basal, but in all cases, children have access to books. They have been matched to books they can handle independently with some ease, or they are rereading books that have previously been introduced. Everyone is reading.

Sometimes during independent reading, I see several pairs of children "buddy reading" to accommodate children who need the support of reading with someone else. The teacher may allow pairs that work well to stay together for a long time when this practice supports extensive reading.

One model has third graders forming book clubs later in the year once they have "proven themselves" in independent reading. The third graders get together with three or four of their friends, choose what to read, and decide how to respond, read, discuss, and make assignments. Often the clubs are "ability grouped" by what the readers can do. The clubs are dynamic social interactions. *Who* children read with in these clubs is often more important to them than *what* they read. The readers are engaged. (Calkins, 1998).

During independent reading, the teacher decides what to do based on the level and needs of the students. The choices include conducting a couple of individual conferences (each lasting about seven minutes), facilitating one or two small reading groups, or a combination of these choices.

In conference, the teacher gets to know the student individually—observing the reader, perhaps conducting a running record with primary readers, checking book bags to make sure the choices match the child, recommending when it's time to exchange an old book for a new one, always teaching, motivating, assessing. She's not necessarily doing something to the reader; she's doing something *for* the reader.

Lucy Calkins says one can tell how effective the reading program is by what is happening during independent reading. "My goal," says Calkins, "is independent reading—to weave reading into the passion, into the fabric of children's lives....independent reading must be the most important part of the day." (Calkins, 1996).

SHARED READING INSTRUCTION   20 MINUTES

Shared reading might form the central role in whole-class instruction in kindergarten and first grade, or the focus might be a phonics lesson. The first-grade teacher might be sharing an enlarged text with the class conducting a mini-lesson. Reading and rereading are present everywhere as the teacher models good reading strategies or leads an activity such as group choral reading for better fluency.

Whole-class instruction during shared reading is teacher-directed and may be focused on comprehension development, literature, or word specific knowledge. Activities vary depending on the grade level and needs of the students: read-alouds and book talks, phonics instruction, word wall work, engaging children with a new piece of literature—a plethora of possibilities exist.

Shared reading is a time when children and teacher read together. The teacher teaches strategies or skills directly and children practice skills during this valuable part of the reading workshop.

GUIDED READING   20 MINUTES

In this segment, the teacher is working with children in a small group. It is a time when readers are presented material at their instructional level and guided so that they can move to greater independence. The rest of the children are working in high-power literacy centers. They are reading!

In one corner of the room, the teacher is meeting with a reading group of four to six students seated around a table. (Since knowing students individually is a priority, the teacher limits the group size to six.) Flexible grouping allows the teacher to form groups to address specific assessed needs and skill levels. You might see teachers conducting a guided reading session with children of common ability. Sometimes children are assembled at the group table with their book bags while the teacher meets with each child individually. Meanwhile, the others in the group are reading independently or responding in their notebooks to something they have read.

What are the rest of the children doing while the teacher meets with small groups? In the back of the classroom is a carpeted area where five children are reading independently. In the center of the room, three pairs of students are buddy reading. Over to the left against the wall behind a partition is the listening center where you might find two children with headsets reading books on tape. Some children are doing follow-up activities to a shared storybook reading session or working on a follow-up activity at a center responding to a book read in class. These reading extensions may be written, dramatic, or artistic responses to books. Two children with pointers are standing in front of a wall covered with a large collection of sentence strips that stretches from the floor as high as the children can reach. The children work on fluency as they practice reading the sentence strips.

Wherever you look, you will see children reading. They can sustain their independent work for twenty minutes while the teacher works with the small group assessing children's reading, demonstrating good reading strategies, and providing opportunities for practice and response.

All three segments of the reading workshop create a favorable environment to support reading. The teacher has matched children with the right books, provided access to books, engaged, nudged, and motivated the readers. Children in this schedule understand the importance of time spent reading during the school day.

I also like an alternative research-based schedule being used by the Balanced Early Literacy project (Hill and Crévola, 2000). In this schedule, the one-hour reading block is structured within a three-part whole-class/small-group/whole-class framework as presented below.

DAILY BEL (Balanced Early Literacy) READING WORKSHOP

WHOLE-CLASS FOCUS   15 minutes

The daily reading workshop, a teacher-directed time, begins with a whole-class focus that is based on the shared reading strategy. Shared reading can consist of books, charts, poems, songs, etc. At upper levels, this segment may be a read-aloud and book talk. The whole-class focus of the classroom program sets the scene for the workshop, providing an initial teaching focus and specific teaching of the visual information of print, including direct instruction in phonics.

SMALL-GROUP TEACHING FOCUS   40 minutes

The longest section of the reading workshop focuses on the explicit teaching of small groups of students. The strategies of reading to children, language experience, Directed-Reading-Thinking Activities, and guided reading take place at the same time that literacy centers are in operation for the remainder of the class. This is a time for students to take responsibility for large sections of their learning time.

WHOLE-CLASS FOCUS: SHARING   5 minutes

The concluding section of the reading workshop is also teacher-directed time. During this time, the teacher encourages the development of students' oral language by giving them the opportunity to reflect on and articulate what they have learned. This shared time draws the workshop to a close and the teacher concludes the formal reading components for the day.

DAILY WRITING WORKSHOP

The writing workshop runs for about 45 minutes. Time spent in each block is flexible depending on the level and needs of the students.

INDEPENDENT WRITING   15 minutes

Children write independently, and expectations and routines are clearly established. During this block, the teacher conducts writing conferences, and depending on the level and needs of students, the teacher has the option to conduct small guided writing groups. If the teacher chooses to do guided writing, children who are not in guided writing are writing independently.

SHARED WRITING INSTRUCTION   15 minutes

Children receive direct instruction. The type and timing of instruction varies with the level and needs of students. Techniques include modeled writing, shared writing, language experience approach for emergent writers, interactive writing, and sometimes guided writing with the whole group.

GUIDED WRITING   15 minutes

Children are in small-group instruction or are writing independently. The teacher meets with small groups and guides students in the process of writing, helping them to develop specific skills or strategies needed by the group.

SPELLING WORKSHOP

For a detailed description of a 15-minute spelling workshop, see Chapter 6.

SNAPSHOTS OF WRITING WORKSHOP

In the Manhattan New School, Sharon Taberski, who follows a format much like the one presented above, says that routines in writing workshop should be predictable and easy to manage. Her writing workshop mirrors her reading workshop—independent writing, shared writing, guided writing, individual conferences, group conferences. Children know what to expect because they use the same routine and the same areas of the classroom for writing workshop as they do for reading workshop. Structure and routines are important elements in the appropriate management of time in writing workshop. For example, children don't sit around wondering what to do if they have a piece of writing to edit. There's a wall chart to guide the second-grade writers through a self-edit:

1. Read what you wrote. Does it make sense?
2. Circle misspelled words.
3. Correct as many as you can.
4. End sentences with . ? !
5. Put capital letters in important places.

Taberski uses other routines. The same story map used to conceptualize stories read aloud or stories read in reading workshop is used to create new stories in writing workshop:

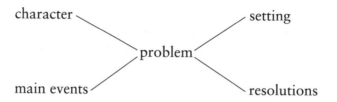

(Taberski, 1997).

Time in writing workshop is spent writing. In addition to spending time with the teacher in writing conferences, guided writing groups, and shared writing, writing workshop is a time for extensive independent writing. A fairly common writing workshop format has children listing topics, choosing one, writing a draft, putting in details, revising with a friend, editing the piece, submitting it for teacher editing, and then moving on to the next piece.

Lucy Calkins believes one more authentic way to connect writing to children's lives is to encourage writing that evolves from a writer's notebook. Children keep a writer's notebook as a rehearsal or seed out of which major writing grows. To start the writer's notebook, children gather five to twenty entries by the end of the first week, writing every night and in writer's workshop. Then they read over the entries and pick one that means something to them. They write around that topic for a period of time. Their choice places investment in a topic.

Time spent writing is critical to the success of this procedure. Once writers choose a topic to develop in their writer's notebook, they are expected to write about the topic in eight or ten pieces. The point is, they have to write a lot around that topic. These pieces might be juxtaposed, put together, crossed out, and developed into a significant piece of writing. (Calkins, 1996).

These procedures work because children must keep up with the volume. They have a huge investment of time spent writing. Again, it's about time. Classrooms where many children develop as writers and meet writing benchmarks on the literacy map are likely to be those where major investments of time in writing workshop and other independent writing activities enable children to spend time writing.

Spelling workshop is a commitment of time to develop word specific knowledge and good spelling habits. With spelling, I believe the consideration of time is different from that of reading or writing. Best instructional practice limits spelling instruction to about 15 minutes per day. Often, time spent on spelling falls into extremes: too much spelling time or not enough. We will look at an efficient process model for spelling workshop in Chapter 6.

The BEL configuration for the one-hour writing workshop subsumes the spelling workshop, and like the schedule presented above, it is a mirror of the reading workshop schedule. In the BEL context, we again see a three-part, whole-class/small-group/whole-class structure integrating modeled writing, shared writing, language-experience approach, interactive writing where teacher and students share the pen, guided writing, and independent writing. (Hill and Crévola, 2000).

DAILY BEL WRITING WORKSHOP

WHOLE-CLASS FOCUS   15 minutes

The daily writing workshop begins with a whole-class focus which consists of either modeled writing or shared writing.

SMALL-GROUP TEACHING FOCUS   40 minutes

During this section of the writing workshop, the teaching strategies of language experience, interactive writing, and guided writing take place while the remainder of the class is engaged in independent writing and various other activities included to extend the students' understanding of grammar and spelling.

WHOLE-CLASS FOCUS: SHARING   5 minutes

The concluding section of the writing workshop offers a time for reflection and an opportunity for children to share what they have learned.

At the beginning of this chapter, I asked you to stand in the doorway of your classroom and ask, "How are children spending their time? Are they reading independently 45 minutes everyday? Are they writing 45 minutes everyday? Do children in my classroom spend time with spelling—finding words, inspecting words, mastering words, and developing better spelling habits?"

Do this mental exercise often. Ask the same questions about how each student spends his or her time as you get to know your students individually.

HOW ARE YOU SPENDING *YOUR* TIME?

I believe the literacy map helps teachers monitor their own success in balancing time wisely and completing the tasks required to teach literacy successfully. If you are confident that you know specifically the desired learning outcomes and have a good sense of how children should be spending their time, it's easier to determine the big jobs you should be doing when teaching reading. I used this notion to construct a checklist that I've used with teachers to monitor their own success. Give yourself a gold star for each job if you are certain you are getting the job done!

BIG JOBS THAT EARN YOU SEVEN GOLD STARS

The following seven-point job list will help you determine if you can give yourself a gold star for each job.

✓ **Match children with books.** This is one of the most important jobs of the reading teacher, because your students need practice reading at a level that is not too hard. You'll find specific guidelines for matching children with books on page 75. If you have book bags and/or leveled text in your classroom, it's often a good sign that you are matching children with books.

✓ **Teach comprehension.** Making meaning with words is the key to reading. One sign that you are earning a gold star in this category is that you are using read-alouds as vehicles for conducting book talks (i.e., think-alouds) that model how good readers think. It's powerful to read aloud to your students, because you "make meaning." When you read aloud and when children read aloud, you must model comprehension strategies. Are you modeling how to make text-to-self, text-to-text, and text-to-world knowledge connections during conferences, read-alouds, or guided reading?

Are you using Directed-Reading-Thinking Activities (DRTA's) to show readers how to make and confirm predictions? Are your students making predictions and reading ahead to find out what's going to happen next? If all this sounds familiar, give yourself a gold star!

✓ **Teach decoding—kindergarten through grade 3 teachers.** Phonics *is* important but not *the* answer! If all you do is teach phonics, you're in trouble and so are your students, because your teaching isn't balanced. There is no question, however, that you do teach use of spelling/sound strategies.

All readers use phonics as a strategy for figuring out unknown words. Pay attention to the type and timing of phonics instruction. The end-of-grade benchmarks help keep you on track as to how much time you need to devote to phonics. Much of the knowledge of regular phonics patterns should be learned before the end of first grade. It is extended in second grade but not a major benchmark category for grade three. Much of first and second-grade spelling instruction is phonics. Third-grade teachers teach some phonics in spelling lessons, but teachers who spend an inordinate amount of time on phonics with third-grade-level readers should not give themselves a gold star.

✓ **Teach fluency.** The teaching of fluency is too often omitted from reading instruction. Fluency is important at all levels but particularly in kindergarten, first, and second grades. Model Fluency by reading aloud. Teach fluency with enlarged text in shared reading. At emergent levels, encourage lots of rereading. Have children practice sections of text until they can read them with fluency. Build fluency by reading along with a tape recorder.

✓ **Teach word specific knowledge.** Accomplish this by teaching spelling, vocabulary, and sight word recognition for emerging readers. Fifteen minutes a day of spelling instruction in grades two and three and using word walls are examples of activities that earn you a gold star in this category. Teachers who read aloud to model academic language and teachers who teach vocabulary are teaching word specific knowledge. Of course, word specific knowledge is also increased by independent reading.

✓ **Engage children as readers.** What do you do in your classroom to make children love reading? If lots of things come to mind, give yourself a gold star. I often see teachers engaging children as readers by reading aloud. Nothing is more powerful! You engage children as readers when whatever you are doing makes them want to read.

✓ **Have high expectations.** You must get them to read! Give yourself a gold star if the following statement describes your attitude: "In my class, you must read. I'll give you a book that is not too hard, that's my job. Your job is to read. I'll make reading fun. I'll make reading interesting. But reading in my classroom is required!"

These are the seven jobs of a good reading teacher. I hope you earned gold stars for all seven!

Remember Vicky Velasquez and the pep squad cheers? The key to literacy success for children like Vicky is not to be found in gimmicks, but it is often found when their time is spent wisely. Engaging children in reading, writing, spelling, and small group instruction works. It's about time!

CHAPTER 4

KINDERGARTEN LITERACY MAP

ASSESSMENT AND TEACHING ACTIVITIES

The kindergarten literacy map is presented as 11 essential literacy requirements. If the benchmarks for each of these areas are achieved, the child has the requisite knowledge and skills needed for success in first grade.

ELEVEN ESSENTIAL ELEMENTS OF KINDERGARTEN LITERACY

Listening Comprehension
Exposure to Print
Reading Comprehension
Phonemic Awareness
Knowledge of the Alphabet
Beginning Phonics Knowledge
Word Specific Knowledge
Writing
Spelling
Ideas and World Knowledge
Attitudes about Reading and Writing

I recommend formal benchmark checks in September, January, and May. These checks allow you to monitor each child and the effectiveness of your teaching. The September check allows you to establish starting points of instruction for each individual. If children come to kindergarten already having met some of the kindergarten benchmarks, you will be able to raise your expectations for those students. (See kindergarten and first-grade checklists on pages 130-139.)

The midyear, or January, check informs your instruction for the remainder of the year and allows you to plan, teach, and assess more efficiently and effectively. Assessment should be ongoing in order to constantly inform your teaching.

The May check allows you to trace each individual's growth and to record specific achievement in light of the goals you set in September. This final check is designed to help you answer a number of important questions about each individual:

- Has the child successfully negotiated the kindergarten literacy map?
- Have the benchmark standards for kindergarten been met, ensuring that the child is ready to take the next step on the literacy map?
- Is work needed over the summer? In what areas is summer work most critical?
- To what degree is this child prepared for success with literacy in first grade?

ASSESSMENT AND TEACHING ACTIVITIES

Feedback is one of the most important functions of assessment. In his book, *Greater Expectations*, William Damon provides the following reminder that good teaching begins with assessment.

Because assessment always reflects standards, and because standards are central to the very mission of schooling, *it is essential that the practice of assessment be considered at the outset* as an integral, defining component of the school's instructional program. (Damon, 1995, p. 208)

Now that you have the map of literacy expectations for kindergarten— 28 specific benchmarks organized under 11 essential literacy requirements—evaluating each child is relatively easy. Following are assessment tips and ways to get feedback, as well as specific teaching activities to help your students meet benchmarks in each of the 11 essential areas.

In Chapter 2 we saw how important it is for children to write regularly and how much information about an individual's literacy development can be determined from observing and analyzing children's writing. I recommend you start September observations by looking closely at children's writing or writing approximations. *When children write, you can see what they need to learn.* Collect a representative sample of each child's writing or writing approximations and check it against each of the kindergarten/first-grade benchmarks to establish a baseline. Keep this question in mind: "What does this writing sample tell me about this child's baseline for this particular benchmark?" After your assessment, conduct a brief interview with the child to complete your baseline assessment.

STEP ONE: Study a writing sample to see what information it gives you about the benchmarks. Conduct a brief interview to ask questions about the sample and have the student read the writing sample out loud.
When **Step One** is completed, proceed to **Step Two** on page 41.

Here are three samples of writing or writing approximations collected in September. Let's see how they inform us about what each child needs to learn.

Antonio's Sample. The following sample was collected from Antonio on September 10. His teacher conducted a brief interview to ask him about his writing.

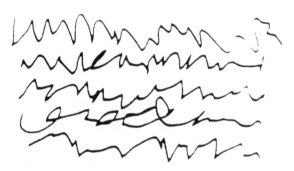

Figure 4.1 *Scribbling—Antonio*

Antonio's writing sample shows a child who has limited experience with print. Some teachers consider children who begin kindergarten scribbling, with little or no knowledge of the alphabet, to be "at risk." They plan for more intervention or more time spent teaching these children letter knowledge, sounds, and the alphabet principle. This writing sample allows the teacher to establish a baseline and date for kindergarten benchmarks 13, 14, 15, 16, 17, 19, 20, 21, 22, 23 and 24.

KNOWLEDGE OF THE ALPHABET	Not Yet	Some/Sometimes	All/Always
K-13. Recites the letters of the alphabet	✓ 9/1		
K-14. Recognizes and names most of the upper-case and lowercase letters of the alphabet (Use the checklist on page 153.)	✓ 9/1		
K-15. Writes independently most of the upper-case and lowercase letters of the alphabet (Use the checklist on page 155.)	✓ 9/1		

BEGINNING PHONICS KNOWLEDGE	Not Yet	Some/Sometimes	All/Always
K-16. Understands the alphabet principle, that the sequence of letters in a written word represents the sequence of sounds (phonemes) in a spoken word	✓ 9/1		
K-17. Corresponds sound to the letters of the alphabet	✓ 9/1		

WRITING	Not Yet	Stage 1	Beyond Stage 1
K-19. Draws a picture that tells a story and approximates writing by labeling the picture or writing about the picture using Stage 1 spelling (Note: This is a midyear kindergarten benchmark.)	✓ 9/1		

	Not Yet	Stage 2	Beyond Stage 2
K-20. Draws a picture that tells a story and approximates writing by labeling the picture or writing about the picture using Stage 2 spelling (Note: This is an end of kindergarten year benchmark.)	✓ 9/1		
K-21. Uses the convention of leaving a space between words (Note: This is an end of kindergarten year benchmark.)	✓ 9/1		

SPELLING	Not Yet	Stage 1	Beyond Stage 1
K-22. Attempts to write or label using random letters for spelling (Note: This is Stage 1, Pre-communicative spelling. It is "the babbling level of spelling," and a midyear kindergarten benchmark.)	✓ 9/1		

	Not Yet	Stage 2	Beyond Stage 2
K-23. Spells words by matching some of the sounds in the words with an appropriate letter correspondence, such as KT for cat, BDA for birthday, or EKFH for egg. (Note: This is Stage 2, Semiphonetic spelling. It is the "abbreviated spelling," and an end of kindergarten year benchmark.)	✓ 9/1		

	Not Yet	Some/Sometimes	All/Always
K-24. Spells and writes his/her first name correctly	✓ 9/1		

While all of Antonio's assessment resulted in "not yet," it was a powerful commentary indicating where he was on the kindergarten literacy map and where he needed to go. One could assume that given Antonio's lack of experience with print, many of the remaining 17 benchmarks, which could easily be observed or assessed in class, might also be "not yet." The message and challenge for Antonio's teacher in September is a clear one: "Let's get to work!" But teaching Antonio literacy is far from an insurmountable task. And this task will be easier, because the kindergarten literacy map shows us exactly where Antonio needs focus.

Leslie's Sample. Leslie has created strings of letters in rows and can "read" her writing. It says "a flock of butterflies."

Figure 4.2 *Leslie's Description of Butterflies*

The teacher collected this sample from Leslie on September 8 and conducted a five-minute interview. Here are her findings:

From the September 8 interview and writing sample, Leslie's teacher was able to establish a baseline for 17 of the 28 kindergarten benchmarks. Leslie was already becoming literate. It would be delightful to watch her journey across the literacy map continue to unfold during the next nine months of kindergarten.

LISTENING COMPREHENSION	Not Yet	Some/Sometimes	All/Always
K-2. Retells stories or parts of stories			
Comment or give examples: *Leslie recounted a wonderful story about* *the flock of butterflies. Remarkable oral* *responses during book talks following read-* *alouds in class.*			✓ 9/8

EXPOSURE TO PRINT	Not Yet	Some/Sometimes	All/Always
K-4. Understands the concept of word (i.e., realizes that speech can be recorded in words; realizes what a printed word is)		✓ 9/8	

PHONEMIC AWARENESS	Not Yet	Some/Sometimes	All/Always
K-10. Understands that words are composed of speech sounds (e.g., *back* /b/ + /ak/)		✓ 9/8	

KNOWLEDGE OF THE ALPHABET	Not Yet	Some/Sometimes	All/Always
K-13. Recites the letters of the alphabet			✓ 9/8
K-14. Recognizes and names most of the uppercase and lowercase letters of the alphabet (Use the checklist on page 153.)		✓ 9/8	
K-15. Writes independently most of the uppercase and lowercase letters of the alphabet (Use the checklist on page 155.)	✓ 9/8		

BEGINNING PHONICS KNOWLEDGE	Not Yet	Some/Sometimes	All/Always
K-16. Understands the alphabet principle, that the sequence of letters in a written word represents the sequence of sounds (phonemes) in a spoken word	✓ 9/8		
K-17. Corresponds sound to the letters of the alphabet	✓ 9/8		

WRITING	Not Yet	Stage 1	Beyond Stage 1
K-19. Draws a picture that tells a story and approximates writing by labeling the picture or writing about the picture using Stage 1 spelling (Note: This is a midyear kindergarten benchmark.)			✓ 9/8

	Not Yet	Stage 2	Beyond Stage 2
K-20. Draws a picture that tells a story and approximates writing by labeling the picture or writing about the picture using Stage 2 spelling (Note: This is an end of kindergarten year benchmark.)	✓ 9/8		
K-21. Uses the convention of leaving a space between words (Note: This is an end of kindergarten year benchmark.)	✓ 9/8		

SPELLING	Not Yet	Stage 1	Beyond Stage 1
K-22. Attempts to write or label using random letters for spelling (Note: This is Stage 1, Pre-communicative spelling. It is "the babbling level of spelling," and a midyear kindergarten benchmark.)		✓ 9/8	

SPELLING	Not Yet	Stage 2	Beyond Stage 2
K-23. Spells words by matching some of the sounds in the word with an appropriate letter correspondence, such as KT for cat, BDA for birthday, or EKFH for egg. (Note: This is Stage 2, Semiphonetic spelling. It is the "abbreviated spelling," and an end of kindergarten year benchmark.)	✓ 9/8		

	Not Yet	Some/Sometimes	All/Always
K-24. Spells and writes his/her first name correctly			✓ 9/8

IDEAS AND WORLD KNOWLEDGE	Not Yet	Some/Sometimes	All/Always
K-25. Expresses ideas, thinks creatively, and organizes information in ways that are appropriate for kindergarten Comment or give examples: _____ _____ _____ _____ _____			✓ 9/8
K-26. Demonstrates age appropriate world knowledge Comment or give examples: *Superior for kindergartner. Her use of "flock"* *in the story is one example of her extensive* *vocabulary.* _____ _____			✓ 9/8

ATTITUDES ABOUT READING AND WRITING	Not Yet	Some/Sometimes	All/Always
K-28. Chooses writing related activities for enjoyment Comment or give examples: *Leslie loves to write!* _____ _____ _____			✓ 9/8

Michael's Sample. Michael entered kindergarten with many beginning first-grade literacy skills. The September Baseline Benchmark Check and interview revealed that he already had reached 20 kindergarten benchmarks (Benchmarks 1, 2, 3, 4, 5, 9, 10, 13, 16, 18, 19, 20, 21, 22, 23, 24, 25, 26, 27, 28) and that he had partially met four benchmarks (Benchmarks 11, 14, 15, 17). Michael's teacher planned to do an extended benchmark check with the first-grade benchmark checklist to set Michael's baselines and to formulate a plan to support Michael's journey on the literacy map. Because he is ready, Michael would be given opportunities to explore an expanded and advanced curriculum in kindergarten that includes many first-grade literacy benchmarks.

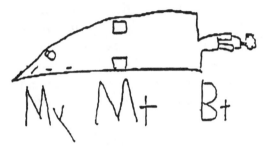

Figure 4.3 *"My Motor Boat" Michael Kindergarten (a Stage 2 speller)*

STEP TWO: Some benchmarks cannot be assessed from the writing sample. After completing **Step One**, go through each of the remaining benchmarks on page 130 taking each of the 11 essential literacy requirements in order. (The following section provides assessment strategies and teaching activities for each of the 11 essential literacy requirements of kindergarten.)

ASSESS LISTENING COMPREHENSION

Every day, a reading/writing kindergarten provides numerous opportunities for the teacher to assess listening comprehension by observing and interviewing each child in the classroom. Assess after read-alouds and storytelling and during individual conferences with children. Here are some informal ways of assessing comprehension:

- Observe children as they respond to the text.
- Talk with children about the material read.
- Ask children to tell about where the story happened.

- Ask children to describe one main character.
- Ask children to describe what happened in the story.

To assess comprehension more formally, you might keep anecdotal records to document information gained through observation and conversation. You might have children retell the story in sequence and tape-record or transcribe the retelling. The retelling could be analyzed to assess understanding of setting, character recall and development, events, and plot.

ASSESS EXPOSURE TO PRINT

The organization of your classroom and your schedule greatly impact the ease of benchmark assessment, and ensure the likelihood that children will meet kindergarten goals. Specific recommendations from the March 18, 1998 report, *Preventing Reading Difficulties in Young Children* (a U.S. government-sponsored report by prominent reading experts assembled by the National Research Council), highlight the need, as early as kindergarten, for "environments that promote language, literacy growth, and skills identified as predictors of later reading achievement."

Accordingly, to maximize students' capabilities, kindergarten instruction should be designed to accomplish the following:
- Stimulate verbal interaction
- Enrich vocabularies
- Encourage talk about books
- Provide practice texts, including materials that challenge appropriately in the areas of vocabulary, linguistic, rhetorical, or conceptual structure.
(*Reading Today,* April/May 1998, p. 4)

A reading/writing kindergarten classroom is your first line of defense for helping children meet benchmarks and for conducting ongoing assessment through daily observations of children reading, writing, and spelling. When you watch children read or approximate reading, you see what they need to learn. Likewise, you see where children are on the literacy map when they listen to read-aloud stories and respond, when they write or approximate writing, and when they spell or invent spellings.

How do we create these environments? Begin with a reading/writing kindergarten schedule similar to those shown on pages 25-31. Scheduling and observing children during shared and guided reading, writing, spelling, and listening to read-alouds allows daily, ongoing assessment. Time should be afforded for adults conversing with children and children conversing with each other. Books are read, and the teacher and children talk about the content of the books. Each child's knowledge of the world, story structure, concept of word, and vocabulary are expanded by read-alouds and book talk.

Language-rich environments promote the language skills children must develop for literacy. Children in a reading/writing kindergarten learn about the alphabetic principle and learn that reading is about finding meaning. They begin to acquire fluency through practice with easy reading materials that the teacher models and rereads, engaging students in shared reading and other reading activity. In this context, the teacher assesses children's development each day. (For more information on assessment, see *An Observation Survey* by Marie Clay (1993). Portsmouth, NH: Heinemann.) Alternative models for a kindergarten schedule may be found in *Classrooms that Work* by Patricia M. Cunningham and Richard L. Allington (1994). New York: HarperCollins Publishers pp. 205-217).

TEACHING ACTIVITY: SHARED READING

Select a big book, poem, or language experience chart appropriate for kindergartners. If you select a big book, read the short blurb (on the back cover) or tell children enough about the story to create anticipation. Allow them to make mental hypotheses regarding the content of the book. Discuss the parts of the book.

Here's a great book that you can learn to read. Its by Bill Martin, Jr. Look at the front cover. What do you see in the picture? That's right. It's a brown bear. Let's look on the back cover. What do you see? Yes. It's the back of a brown bear. It's funny how the author put the bear's front on the front cover and the back view of the bear on the back cover. Can you help me find the title? Here it is. The title of this book is Brown Bear, Brown Bear, What Do You See? *Watch as I read the title and point to the words.*

Brown Bear, Brown Bear, What Do You See?
(Point to each word, making the voice print match.)

Now, you read it with me.
That's great. You just read the title!
Let's try that again.

After everyone rereads the title in unison, the teacher reads the book aloud pointing to the words with a pointer. Sometimes she stops and asks children to predict what will happen next with questions such as "What animal do you think the bear will see on the next page?" She keeps the children engaged with the story. After children are familiar with the story and story pattern, the teacher conducts a shared reading lesson. The children join the teacher reading aloud in unison from the enlarged text as the teacher points to the words. The teacher models concepts of print such as holding the book correctly, turning pages from left to right, relating pictures to content, making the voice match the print, and understanding directionality. She uses words and phrases to build concepts of print and to help children understand the reading process.

Following are two activities for making books. By making their own books, children develop concepts about print—the parts of a book, pages are turned left to right, clusters of letters form words, and the print tells the story.

TEACHING ACTIVITY: KEEP BOOKS

I like the concept of Keep Books, inexpensive homemade books that children keep and read at home. The idea is not to replace children's literature but to increase children's reading at home. Keep Book Programs, such as the one sponsored by Ohio State University and reported by Fountas and Pinnell in *Guided Reading* (1996), greatly increase a young child's exposure to books.

Figure 4.4 *The layout of a typical Keep Book.*

TEACHING ACTIVITY: MAKING AN EIGHT-PAGE BOOK
FROM ONE SHEET OF PAPER

Regie Routman includes this activity in her teaching resource *Invitations* (1994). I include it here because it's such a powerful concept for increasing children's exposure to books.

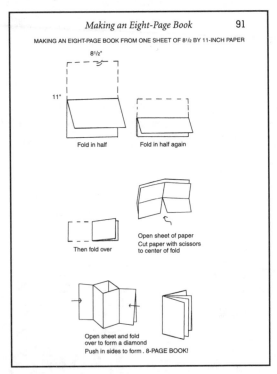

Figure 4.5 *Instructions to make an eight-page book*

ASSESS READING COMPREHENSION

The end of year benchmark for kindergarten is that kindergartners approximate reading and actually engage in some real reading. They should be able to look at pictures in familiar text and talk about the content. They should also be able to look at pictures in unfamiliar text and make resonable hypotheses about the content.

Kindergartners should read a few pattern books or easy-to-read books from memory. In the first half of kindergarten these books may have two or three words per page and are written in phrases with no structure changes. Examples include nursery rhymes, alphabet books, pop-up books, board books, and concept books such as colors, animals, numbers, shapes, etc. By the end of kindergarten, children should draw upon predictable language patterns, recognize some sight words, and engage in actual reading of text at levels A and B (see page 162).

> Books at this level provide strong links to experiences of young children who are learning to read through the use of familiar concepts and vocabulary, commonly used oral-language patterns, repetition of those patterns, and illustrations that closely portray the meaning and language of the story. These books generally have one line of text and are written in sentence form with no change in structure. (Independent Reading Guide, 1997, p. 13)

To assess whether kindergartners can read books at this level, choose benchmark books that fit this description such as *Honk!* by Sue Smith. Keep records of which books at this level the kindergarten child can read and comprehend.

Honk! by Sue Smith
Level B *Guided Reading* (Fountas and Pinnell, 1996)

The Reading Comprehension benchmark can be assessed through daily observation. Some teachers begin taking running records of kindergarten readers. A sample of a kindergarten running record is presented in Figure 4.6. A running record blank, and a scoring sheet for retelling to further assess comprehension following a running record, are provided on pages 151-152.

Figure 4.6

RUNNING RECORD

Name_____ Date_____

Analysis of Errors and Self Corrections

Easy ✓ Instructional ☐ Challenging ☐	M Meaning
	S Structure
	V Visual

Page #	Title/Text *Run! Run!* Text Reading Level **C** Seen Text ☐ Unseen Text ☐	# of E	# of SC	INFORMATION USED	
				Error Analysis M S V	Self Correction Analysis M S V
1	✓✓ Run! Run!				
2	✓✓✓✓ The three pigs ran away				
	✓✓✓ from the wolf.				
3	✓✓✓ Run, pigs, run!				
	✓✓✓✓✓ The wolf wants to eat you.	1		ⓂS V	
4	✓✓✓ Jack ran away				
	✓✓ man|SC̶ from the giant. g̶i̶a̶n̶t̶				
5	✓✓✓ Run, Jack, run!				
	✓✓✓✓✓✓The giant wants to eat you.				
6	✓✓✓✓ Red Riding Hood ran away				
	✓✓✓ from the wolf.				
7	✓✓✓ Run, Red, run!				
	✓✓✓✓✓The wolf wants to eat you.				
8	✓✓✓✓✓✓ Cinderella ran away from the prince.				
	✓✓✓ Stop, Cinderella, stop!				
	✓✓✓✓✓✓The prince wants to kiss you.				

Adapted from Marie Clay. *The Early Detection of Reading Difficulties* (Heinemann).

ASSESSMENT ACTIVITY: RUNNING RECORDS

Running records, developed by Marie Clay (1993), is a technique to assess children's oral reading and comprehension. I like this technique because, once you know the procedure, you can easily use it with any book a child is reading. It's a structured way of recording which strategies the reader is using and requires only a blank sheet of paper to check off each word read correctly or record what the student says that is different from the text. Scoring conventions are provided below.

Conventions for Recording Running Records

1. Use a check mark (✔) to indicate every word read correctly.

2. If a child reads incorrectly, the child's word is written above a horizontal line, and the word in the text is written below the line.
   Child: *gray*
   Text: *great*   (One error)

3. Record all of a child's attempts to read a word.
   Child: *gray gr---- grass*
   Text: *green*   (One error)

   Child: *gr gree green*
   Text: *green*   (No error)

4. If a child succeeds in correcting an error, record as self-correction (SC).
   Child: *gray great SC*
   Text: *green*   (No error)

5. If a child omits a word, a dash is recorded over the line.
   Child: ——
   Text: *green*   (One error)

6. If a child inserts a word, the inserted word is written over the line, and a dash is recorded under the line.
   Child: *great*
   Text: ——   (One error)

7. If the child is unable to proceed, he or she is told the word (T).   (One error)

8. When a child appeals for help, he is asked to try again before telling him as in item 7.
   Child —— *A great*
   Text: *green* —— T   (One error)

9. If a child gets confused, he is told to "Try that again," and TTA is marked on the record.   (One error— only the second attempt is scored)

10. Repetition is sometimes used to confirm a previous attempt, often resulting in self-correction.

Child: *In the great gray room* R SC

Text: *In the great green room*   (No error)

Steps to Conduct a Running Record

Step 1: Take a running record similar to the sample above.

Step 2: Score the running record. Count all the words in the book or passage, excluding the title. This gives the running words. Subtract the number of errors from the total number of running words. Divide the remainder by the number of running words. Multiply by 100 to get a percentage.

$$\frac{\text{Running words} - \text{Errors}}{\text{Running words}} \; \text{X} \; 100 = \underline{\hspace{1.5cm}} \; \%$$

Independent   95% or above
(If the percentage is 95% or above, the text is at the child's independent level.)

Instructional   90-94%
(If the percentage is 90-94%, the text is at the child's instructional level.)

Too hard   89% or below
(If the percentage is 89% or below, the text is too hard.)

Step 3: Note appropriate and inappropriate reading strategies
(See activities below.)

Step 4: Further assess comprehension with comprehension questions or by conducting a retelling.

ASSESSMENT ACTIVITY: BENCHMARK BOOKS

For each child, take a running record of two or three books. List those books the child is able to read independently. See Figure 5.2 on page 75 for guidelines for establishing instructional reading criteria. The following books provide information about running records and miscue analysis: Clay, Marie M. *An Observation Survey of Early Literacy Achievement* (Heinemann); Goodman, Yetta, Dorothy Watson, and Carolyn Burke. *Reading Miscue Inventory: Alternative Procedures*. (Richard C. Owen).

TEACHING ACTIVITY: READ-ALOUDS AND MODELING READING

Don't underestimate the power of read-alouds and book talks interspersed with direct teaching. Do them often! In kindergarten, children learn to identify the front of the book, its cover and title, how to hold the book correctly, how to turn the pages left-to-right, how to relate pictures to content, and aspects of directionality from teachers who read aloud, conduct book talks, and discuss each of these features in class. Kindergarteners learn how readers think as they read topic- and text-specific information. Simultaneously, they gain knowledge of story structure, new vocabulary, and academic language.

TEACHING ACTIVITY: LANGUAGE EXPERIENCE APPROACH (LEA)

Language experience approach (Allen, 1976) is an excellent procedure for teaching all aspects of reading including reading comprehension. It can be a natural part of the everyday activity in the kindergarten classroom and a mainstay for small group and guided reading in kindergarten. The teacher takes down dictation of what children say on large charts that become the content of reading lessons and practice.

LEA reading material is meaningful because what is being read is the language and experience of the children doing the reading. The approach provides many opportunities for developing fluency and word recognition, and for modeling concepts of print as well as the concept that what can be said can be written and read back.

Language experience dictation may be labels, sentences, lists, directions, stories or charts summarizing any important kindergarten activity.

ASSESS PHONEMIC AWARENESS

Phonemic awareness is the ability to segment sounds in words. The expectation or desired learning outcome for the end of the kindergarten year is that children will be able to segment some of the sounds of words in initial, medial, and final positions. Segmentation of all of the sounds in words, or complete phonemic awareness, is a midyear first-grade benchmark and occurs along with the midyear first-grade Stage 3 spelling benchmark. Children who produce Stage 3 spelling demonstrate full phonemic awareness, since by definition, Stage 3 phonetic spelling represents all the speech sounds in words.

Since full phonemic awareness is a middle of first grade benchmark, don't expect full phonemic awareness by the end of kindergarten. The kindergarten benchmark is met if your observations allow you to check "Sometimes" for items K-6.—K-8. on the kindergarten checklist.

Phonemic awareness has nothing to do with letters, though once children start using letters to invent spellings and move to Stage 2, semiphonetic spelling (e.g., KT for cat and BDA for birthday), knowing the letters and using them to invent Stage 2 spellings advances phonemic awareness. Children may start by getting only the first letter to match the sound in the words being spelled. Later they will use appropriate letters to match other sounds in medial and final positions as in HMT DPD for *Humpty Dumpty*. Thus, practice with inventing spellings leads kindergartners to consciously try to hear the sounds in words so they can match letters to the sounds. Invented spelling, then, is an excellent way to further develop phonemic awareness. Phonemic awareness may be assessed indirectly by observing children's invented spelling in their writing as demonstrated with the samples earlier in this chapter. Each of the teaching activities described below allows for ample daily observational assessment.

TEACHING ACTIVITY: FOCUS ON A SPECIFIC SOUND

Focus first on initial consonants because they are the easiest to perceive. Find a familiar story, poem, or big book that focuses on a specific sound. Display the text on a chart.

Betty Botter

Betty Botter bought some butter,
But, she said, this butter's bitter;
If I put it in my batter,
It will make my batter bitter,
But a bit of better butter
Will make my batter better.
Bought a bit of better butter.

Anonymous

Read the text. Have children raise their hands each time they hear the target sound. Orally repeat the target words. Have children think of other words that begin with that sound. List children's names that begin with the target sound on a word wall.

TEACHING ACTIVITY: PLAY PHONEMIC AWARENESS GAMES

Ask questions like these:
What word would be left if the *b* sound were taken away from *bat*?
Do *big* and *bike* begin with the same sound?
What word would you have if you put these sounds together:
/b/-/a/-/t/   (*bat*)

What sounds do you hear in *big*?

How many sounds do you hear in *bake*? (three: /b/ /a/ /k/)

Which word starts with a different sound: *bag, nine, beach, bike*?

Is there a /k/ in *bike*?

(Adapted from Keith E. Stanovich, "Romance and Reality" *The Reading Teacher*, January, 1994, p. 283)

ASSESS KNOWLEDGE OF THE ALPHABET

Knowledge of the alphabet is one of the easiest benchmarks to assess, because there are only 26 letters and only three things to know about each of them. (Knowledge of the alphabet principle and knowledge about matching sounds to letters is subsumed under the Beginning Phonics Knowledge benchmark.)

1) How to say letter names at random and in alphabetical order

2) How to recognize uppercase and lowercase letter forms

3) How to write uppercase and lowercase letters.

I know of no easier format than a simple checklist to assess knowledge of the alphabet:

1) A checklist for saying the letters in alphabetical order

2) A checklist for uppercase and lowercase letters arranged in random order. Check each letter as the child names it.

3) Similar checklists to record which letters the kindergartner writes independently (See sample checklists on pages 153-155).

As demonstrated in the beginning of the chapter, a quick and efficient way to begin assessing a child's knowledge of the alphabet is to look at a sample of the child's writing and ask the child a few questions to verify what you construe from the writing sample.

Let's look at our three samples again.

Antonio   Leslie   Michael

At a glance, the three writing samples inform us of each writer's knowledge of the alphabet. One can interpret that Antonio has little, if any, knowledge of the alphabet, Leslie has some knowledge, and Michael probably has extensive knowledge. Watching what children do as they write each day, or observing and noting their response to alphabet instruction in kindergarten would allow one to check the alphabet knowledge benchmark quite easily.

TEACHING ACTIVITY: THE ALPHABET SONG

One of the best ways to teach the alphabet is to teach "The Alphabet Song." The version to the tune of "Twinkle, Twinkle Little Star" is a classic. Try passing out alphabet cards and have "each letter" line up in order as everyone sings the song "in slow motion."

TEACHING ACTIVITY: USING ALPHABET BOOKS

Don't underestimate the importance of alphabet books. Introduce a new alphabet book every couple of weeks. Here are a few of my favorites:

Alligators All Around, by Maurice Sendak (New York: HarperCollins, 1962)

Ashanti to Zulu: African Traditions by Margaret Musgrove, illustrated by Leo and Diane Dillon (New York: Dial Books, 1976)

Aster Aardvark's Alphabet Adventures by Steven Kellogg (New York: Morrow Junior Books, 1987)

Eating the Alphabet: Fruits and Vegetables from A-Z by Lois Ehlert, (San Diego: Harcourt Brace Jovanovich, 1989)

The Dinosaur Alphabet Book by Jerry Pallotta, illustrated by Ralph Masiello (Boston: Charlesbridge, 1990)

The Z Was Zapped by Chris Van Allsburg (Boston: Houghton Mifflin, 1987)

Use big books and collections of alphabet books such as *Alphabet Series* (Mondo Publishing, 1999) to explore letters.

TEACHING ACTIVITY: ALPHABET STRIPS

It's good for kindergartners to see the letters right in front of them rather than always having to look up high on a bulletin board. For easy reference, put a letter strip on each child's desk or in his or her writing folder. Make the alphabet strips about the size of a ruler and list both uppercase and lowercase letters.

Aa Bb Cc Dd Ee Ff ... Zz

ASSESS BEGINNING PHONICS KNOWLEDGE

When children write you can see what they need to learn. This statement should become a mantra for assessment of literacy development. A quick, efficient way to assess a kindergartner's understanding of the alphabet principle (i.e., the sequence of letters in a written word represents the sequence of sounds or phonemes in a spoken word) is to look at how the child uses letters in his or her writing.

Antonio's sample: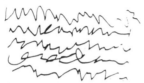

Obviously, Antonio does not have the alphabet principle down pat.

Leslie's sample:

Leslie's random use of letters demonstrates that she does not yet apply the alphabet principle in her writing.

Michael's sample:

When he writes MY MT BT for "my motor boat," Michael demonstrates he knows that the sequence of letters in a written word corresponds to the sequence of sounds in the spoken word. Neither Antonio nor Leslie correspond sound to the letters in their writing, but Michael does indeed correspond sound to some of the letters.

TEACHING ACTIVITY: CONNECTING PHONEMIC AWARENESS TO LETTERS

To help children correspond a sound, such as /b/, to the letter, have them do the following:
- Frame the *b* words in the text.
- Find *b* word items in the classroom, such as *book, bag, box, bulletin board, boys, ball, big books*.
- Draw a scene with *b* words in the picture.
- Prepare a picture chart of items that begin with *b*.

- Label the *b* words on the picture chart.
- Label *b* words in the classroom.
- Model or use shared writing to write a two or three letter *b* word

If writing two or three letter words is a novel activity for your students, have them watch you write the letters and then practice individually. Relate the writing of the *b* word to what students already know, perhaps by choosing a *b* word that most students recognize.

Stretch out the sounds in the word and connect each sound to a letter. After students try to represent each sound, write the correct letter on the chalkboard. Assist students who need help copying the correct letter. Monitor individuals. Assist and provide corrective feedback.

- Find *b* words in several alphabet books and compare entries.
- Add /b/ sound to the class sound book.
- Add *b* words to personal alphabet books.
- Make a chart story with *b* words.
- Read sentence strips and focus on *b* words.
- Read another book or poem with *b* words.

TEACHING ACTIVITY: SOUND AND LETTER BOOKS

Make a Sound and Letter Book for each letter of the alphabet. Have children cut and paste pictures of objects that begin with the target letter. Words recognized from environmental print or children's names beginning with the target letter may be added to the book. Allow children who are ready to label the pictures using Stage 2 or Stage 3 spelling.

TEACHING ACTIVITY: SOUND AND LETTER WORD WALLS

A version of the word wall (presented in Chapter 5) may be used in kindergarten to foster development of phonemic awareness, alphabet knowledge, and beginning phonics knowledge. Follow the general guidelines for developing a word wall beginning on page 88. Keep in mind that the purpose of a word wall in kindergarten is to develop phonemic awareness, knowledge of the alphabet, knowledge of the letter-to-sound match, and recognition of some high frequency words.

- Display the alphabet with space for adding pictures and labels underneath the letters. Focus on a particular letter and conduct word hunts for pictures of objects that begin with that letter.
- Display the pictures with labels. Encourage children to read the word for each picture. Have them listen for the initial sound and name the letter that represents that sound.

- Display children's names on the wall. Have children write, chant, and spell a different name each day.
- Display a few words from environmental print and a few sight words from the kindergarten word wall. (This practice also addresses the Word Specific Knowledge benchmark.)

ASSESS WORD SPECIFIC KNOWLEDGE

Children should leave kindergarten able to recognize *some* words by sight. Monitor sight word recognition in kindergarten informally. In the second half of kindergarten, children might keep word banks comprised of *Words I Can Read* on word cards. In addition to names and words from environmental print, some teachers use a stack of word cards to informally check sight recognition of high frequency words like the ones below. (See also Common Irregularly Spelled Words Checklist on page 158.)

100 HIGH FREQUENCY WORDS

a	fun	me	there
about	get	mother	they
all	go	my	things
and	got	no	this
are	good	not	time
as	going	of	to
at	had	on	too
back	has	one	truck
be	have	or	up
because	he	other	us
big	her	our	very
but	him	out	want
by	his	people	was
came	home	play	we
can	house	said	went
cat	I	saw	were
could	if	school	what
day	n	see	when
did	is	she	will
do	it	so	with
dog	just	some	would
down	like	that	write
for	little	the	you
friends	lot	them	your
from	make	then	zoo

Don't feel compelled to teach a word list. The benchmark for kindergarten is recognition of some words, not recognition of a list of specific words.

Teach word specific knowledge through exposure to print.

Word specific knowledge in kindergarten should be a natural outgrowth of participation in a reading/writing classroom. If you are modeling reading, sharing reading, and children have continued access to books along with opportunities to approximate reading, word specific knowledge will grow. Use the checklist on page 56 to keep track of word specific knowledge.

TEACHING ACTIVITY: WORD WALLS

As children begin to recognize high frequency words in the material they are reading and writing, add them to the word wall. Encourage children to frame the words in books and class writing and to practice writing them.

REVISITING ASSESSMENT OF WRITING AND SPELLING IN KINDERGARTEN

Earlier in this chapter we assessed writing and spelling benchmarks in children's authentic writing or writing approximations. By now you are familiar with assessing Stage 1 and Stage 2 spelling in writing such as those produced by Antonio, Leslie, and Michael. Tips for teaching spelling in kindergarten were presented in this chapter under "Assess Beginning Phonics Knowledge" (see page 54).

In general, limit expectations for correct spelling in kindergarten to the child's name and a few easy sight words that the child learns to spell automatically.

ASSESSMENT ACTIVITY: THE MONSTER TEST

Many kindergarten teachers use "The Monster Test," Gentry's Developmental Spelling Test, (Gentry and Gillet, 1993) for assessment when they observe a classroom of writers at various levels of developmental spelling. (For information on the Developmental Spelling Test, see Chapter 5.)

ASSESS IDEAS AND WORLD KNOWLEDGE

"Ideas and World Knowledge" refers to whether a child expresses ideas, thinks creatively, organizes information appropriate for kindergarten, and demonstrates "appropriate world knowledge." I think this essential element is best assessed informally. In my view, teachers who live within a community of learners in a reading/writing classroom get to know students well enough to assess these benchmarks by observing each child reading, writing, and speaking.

ASSESS ATTITUDES ABOUT READING AND WRITING

The central question in an assessment of attitudes about reading and writing is whether the child engages in stimulating and active performance in these areas. Teachers who know their students, make school useful and interesting, create reading/writing classrooms, and personalize instruction have no difficulty assessing these benchmarks.

I prefer observational assessment of attitudes. Teachers sometimes use inventories or questionnaires to help guide their observation. *Practical Assessments for Literature Based Reading Classrooms* by Adele Fiderer offers sample attitude inventories appropriate for kindergarten.

We began this chapter stating that good teaching begins with assessment. By providing you with concrete and specific kindergarten benchmarks (page 36) and guiding you through a two-step assessment procedure, this chapter has enabled you to track each child's progress on the kindergarten literacy map. Remember to begin your assessment of each child at the outset of kindergarten. Knowing the needs of each individual will empower you as a teacher and will be a defining component of your kindergarten instructional program.

CHAPTER 5

FIRST-GRADE LITERACY MAP

ASSESSMENT AND TEACHING ACTIVITIES

When a child enters first grade, a gateway opens to literacy. This is the year she will *become* literate. It is likely to be the most important year in her academic life.

The first-grade literacy map is presented as 10 essential literacy requirements. If the benchmarks for each of these areas are achieved, the child has the requisite knowledge and skills needed for success in second grade.

TEN ESSENTIAL ELEMENTS OF FIRST-GRADE LITERACY

Listening Comprehension
Exposure to Print
Reading Comprehension
Phonemic Awareness
Knowledge of Regular Phonics Patterns
Word Specific Knowledge
Writing
Spelling
Ideas and World Knowledge
Attitudes about Reading and Writing

These 10 essential areas of development are not necessarily hierarchical. Some areas may develop before others, some areas may develop synergistically, and some may develop in different order. For example, it is well documented that some children write first and some children read first. Keep in mind that the order in which the essential elements are presented in this text is for organizational purposes and does not necessarily reflect the order in which children should acquire them.

I recommend formal benchmark checks in September, January, and May. The September check allows you to establish starting points of instruction for each individual. If children come to first grade lacking some of the kindergarten benchmarks, you will be able to adjust your instruction by adding those kindergarten benchmark goals. (See kindergarten and first-grade checklists on pages 130-139.)

The midyear, or January check (as well as ongoing informal assessment) informs your instruction for the remainder of the year and allows you to plan, teach, and assess more efficiently and effectively. The May check allows you to trace each individual's growth and to record specific achievement in light of the goals you set in September. This final check is designed to help you answer a number of important questions about each individual:

- Has the child successfully negotiated the first-grade literacy map?
- Have the benchmark standards for first grade been met ensuring that the child is ready to take the next step on the literacy map?
- Is work needed over the summer? In what areas is summer work most critical?
- To what degree is this child prepared for success with literacy in second grade?

BENCHMARKS THAT BALANCE FIRST-GRADE LITERACY DEVELOPMENT

Before we go further, let's look at a study of relationships among some key first-grade essential elements—phonemic awareness, knowledge of regular phonics patterns, word specific knowledge and word recognition—reported in *Learning to Read and Write in One Elementary School,* by Connie Juel (1994). Juel's research with first graders is comprehensive and powerful. *Learning to Read and Write in One Elementary School* is a study first-grade teachers should read for themselves. While the study may not be definitive, it provides perspectives on many of the interconnected relationships among factors that must be considered in balanced first-grade literacy instruction.

Juel's model of literacy places importance on phonemic awareness, knowledge of regular phonics patterns, word specific knowledge, and word recognition and shows how these factors contribute to reading comprehension. Her longitudinal studies with first graders predicted relationships among first-grade essential elements. The simplified synthesis of her analysis permits inferences about causal relationships among essential elements of first-grade literacy. (Figure 5.1)

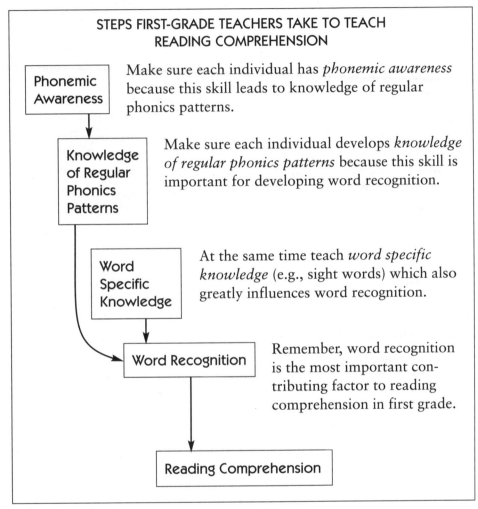

STEPS FIRST-GRADE TEACHERS TAKE TO TEACH READING COMPREHENSION

Phonemic Awareness

Make sure each individual has *phonemic awareness* because this skill leads to knowledge of regular phonics patterns.

Knowledge of Regular Phonics Patterns

Make sure each individual develops *knowledge of regular phonics patterns* because this skill is important for developing word recognition.

Word Specific Knowledge

At the same time teach *word specific knowledge* (e.g., sight words) which also greatly influences word recognition.

Word Recognition

Remember, word recognition is the most important contributing factor to reading comprehension in first grade.

Reading Comprehension

Figure 5.1

When considering the model above, keep in mind that all of the steps in the model should be taken for reading comprehension. You must provide instruction in these areas *along with* exposure to print and comprehension and fluency instruction. Modeled reading, shared reading, and guided reading allow opportunities for the teacher to address all of the essential elements. The benchmark checklist helps the teacher know what specific areas need to be addressed for a particular individual.

The steps presented in the model not only affect reading comprehension, but they affect other essential elements as well. Juel makes this point explicitly.

In particular, a lack of early phonemic awareness severely limits children's growth in cipher knowledge (phonics), which in turn limits their ability to recognize words and to spell, which ultimately acts to constrain growth in listening comprehension and ideas that will in turn limit reading comprehension and writing (1994, p.121).

So, the steps addressed in the model not only impact reading comprehension but listening comprehension, ideas, world knowledge, spelling, and writing.

Juel's study revealed that word recognition in first-grade predicted reading comprehension almost exclusively. In my view, this powerful study shows how the balance in good first-grade instruction may differ from what works well with second and third-grade level learners. In first grade, the factors leading to word recognition receive heavier emphasis. A shift occurs toward the end of first-grade, once children have gained the ability to recognize many words and the ability to handle more sophisticated reading material.

Teachers need to develop an appreciation for the type of instruction that supports children where they are on their particular journey to literacy at a particular time in development. While teachers who work with first-grade-level learners need to place appropriate emphasis on phonemic awareness, regular phonics, and word specific knowledge, the instructional emphasis should be different for learners at higher levels.

The key to balancing instruction in first-grade seems to relate to what Juel calls the "type and timing of instruction" relative to the level of text, or more precisely, relative to the level of the learner. The implications of Juel's study were that first-grade teachers need to make sure children have phonemic awareness by midyear of first grade and that children develop high quality word recognition in first grade. Her major recommendation for the latter was providing children with reading materials in which they can read words with at least 90% accuracy (1994, p. 122).

Juel's study went on to show that predictors of reading comprehension were different at second and third-grade levels when more sophisticated text was in use. By the time children reach these higher levels they must already be recognizing many words and using knowledge of regular phonics to decode many new words. She found factors that influenced whether a child could understand what was spoken out loud, not word recognition, predicted success with reading comprehension at these higher levels. In other words, once the conceptual load and vocabulary became more challenging, listening comprehension played a larger role in predicting whether a child would understand the text (1994, p.123).

The following text samples illustrate what children are expected to read at the beginning and end of first grade.

BEGINNING OF FIRST-GRADE LEVEL

Run! Run! by JoAnn Vandine
(Level C, *Guided Reading*, Fountas and Pinnell, 1996)

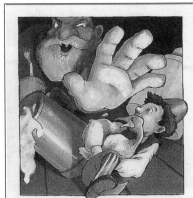

Jack ran away
from the giant.

Run, Jack, run!
The giant wants to eat you.

Red Riding Hood ran away
from the wolf.

Run, Red, run!
The wolf wants to eat you.

Cinderella ran away from the prince.
Stop, Cinderella, stop!
The prince wants to kiss you.

END OF FIRST-GRADE LEVEL

Amelia Bedelia by Peggy Parish
[Level K, *Guided Reading*, Fountas and Pinnell, 1996]

"Oh, Amelia Bedelia,
your first day of work,
and I can't be here.
But I made a list for you.
You do just what the list says,"
said Mrs. Rogers.
Mrs. Rogers got into the car
with Mr. Rogers.
They drove away.

(Text samples are leveled according to guidelines in *Guided Reading: Good First Teaching for All Children* (Irene C. Fountas and Gay Su Pinnell, 1996), which includes an excellent listing of text levels for over 2,500 caption books, natural language texts, and early children's literature.)

What is required to comprehend these texts? In *Run! Run!* little stretch is needed beyond paying attention to the pictures and the patterning of text to achieve full comprehension. *Amelia Bedelia* makes more demands. For example, it exposes the reader to many more running words in the text. Reading this text requires some word recognition and some decoding skill using knowledge of regular phonics patterns. Children without these skills will struggle to comprehend *Amelia Bedelia* when reading independently. This text also allows for more sophisticated text-to-self, text-to-text, and text-to-world knowledge connections.

While there must be a major focus on meaning, the implication for teaching first-grade may be that it is crucial to focus more attention on word recognition and those factors leading to word recognition. In order to negotiate the first-grade literacy map, children must learn to recognize words and decode. (See First-Grade Benchmarks on pages 134-139.) Expect that other factors, such as those that impact how well a child understands what is read aloud, will have greater influence on comprehension at grades two and higher when the conceptual load and vocabulary are more challenging.

Perhaps Juel's study explains why first-grade teachers have found word walls so powerful, and why advocates of a variety of teaching methods agree on the need to teach some sight words in first-grade. The study places phonemic awareness at the start of the first-grade literacy path. This gives credence to many studies that have found phonemic awareness likely to be "critical for achieving the first step in becoming an independent reader." (Juel, 1994, p. 5)

I believe the essential elements highlighted in Figure 5.1 on page 61 must be attended to with all first-grade-level learners, regardless of the teacher's philosophy. In my view, phonemic awareness, knowledge of regular phonics, and word specific knowledge (including word recognition and first-grade-level spelling) must always be considered in the balance of appropriate first-grade-level instruction. All are critical for negotiating the first-grade literacy map.

ASSESSMENT AND TEACHING ACTIVITIES

The big questions in first-grade are, "Is she learning to read?" "Is he learning to write?" " Are they learning to spell?" The benchmark checklist on pages 134-139 and the guidelines in this chapter will help you answer these and other questions about the development of each first grader in your classroom.

The literacy map for first-grade presents 37 specific first-grade benchmarks organized under 10 essential literacy requirements. Because the benchmarks help us know, specifically and concretely, what to look for, information gathering is efficient, relatively effortless, and ongoing. Each minute of the school day provides opportunities to observe and note newly gleaned understandings about each child's placement and progression on the first-grade literacy map. Following are assessment tips and ways to gain feedback for each of the 10 first-grade literacy requirements. There are also teaching activities to help your students meet benchmarks in each of the 10 essential areas. Benchmark assessment should start in September to establish a baseline.

STEP ONE: Study a writing sample for information relevant to the first-grade benchmarks. Have the child read the writing sample aloud. Interview the child to ask questions about the sample and/or to find out more about each benchmark under consideration. Assess as many of the 37 benchmarks as possible from the writing sample and interview.

When **Step One** is completed, proceed to **Step Two** on page 69.

REVISITING JULIE'S "THE THREE LITTLE PIGS"

In Chapter 2 we took **Step One** with one first-grader, Julie, who wrote her own rendition of "The Three Little Pigs." Look again at this writing sample and note how we used it to assess 16 of the 37 first-grade benchmarks and corroborated that assessment in a brief interview.

Step One of Julie's September Baseline Benchmark Check is presented below.

PHONEMIC AWARENESS	Not Yet	Some/Sometimes	All/Always
1-12. Demonstrates phonemic awareness by counting or clapping the number of syllables in a word			✓ 9/30
1-14. Demonstrates full phonemic awareness (Note: Full phonemic awareness is a middle of first-grade benchmark.)			✓ 9/30
KNOWLEDGE OF REGULAR PHONICS PATTERNS	Not Yet	Some/Sometimes	All/Always
1-15. Accurately decodes phonetically regular, one-syllable words (e.g., *web, milk, stamp, bake, boat*)		✓ 9/30	
1-16. Accurately decodes nonsense words such as *dit, nuv, buf, yode, shi, fler,* and *cleef* (Bryant, 1975)		✓ 9/30	
WORD SPECIFIC KNOWLEDGE	Not Yet	Some/Sometimes	Many
1-20. Spells a collection of first-grade-level words correctly (e.g., *the, at, bed, cut, five, green*)		✓ 9/30	

WRITING	Not Yet	Some/Sometimes	Good Variety
1-21. Produces a variety of short compositions (e.g., stories, simple descriptions, journal entries)		✓ 9/30	

	Not Yet	Some/Sometimes	All/Always
1-22. Uses basic punctuation and capitalization	✓ 9/30		

SPELLING	Not Yet	Stage 3	Beyond Stage 3
1-23. Spells words by matching all of the sounds in the word with an appropriate letter correspondence, such as EGL for *eagle*, BOTM for *bottom*, or UNITD for *united* (Note: This is Stage 3, Phonetic spelling. It is "spelling by ear" and a midyear first-grade benchmark.)		✓ 9/30	

	Not Yet	Stage 4	Beyond Stage 4
1-24. Spells words by representing many of the visual aspects of English spelling, such as e-marker pattern, double letters, vowels in all syllables, and vowel digraphs in spellings like EGUL for eagle, BOTUM for bottom, or YOUNIGHTED for united (Note: This is Stage 4, Transitional spelling. It is "spelling by eye," and an end of first-grade benchmark.)	✓ 9/30		

Note: Twenty-two percent of Julie's invented spellings in her "The Three Little Pigs" story *are* transitional which is a good sign that she is moving toward transitional spelling. But she is *not yet* a transitional speller. When more than half of her invented spellings are transitional, she will have met Benchmark 1-24—Spells at Stage 4. (For the developmental analysis of invented spelling in Julie's writing sample see Chapter 2, page 18.)

SPELLING	Not Yet	Some/Sometimes	Many
1-25. Spells many three and four letter phonetically regular, short vowel words correctly (e.g., *bat, sit, milk*)		✓ 9/30	
1-27. Spells some high frequency, irregular sight words correctly (e.g., *of, the, one, have*)		✓ 9/30	

IDEAS AND WORLD KNOWLEDGE	Not Yet	Some/Sometimes	All/Always
1-28. Expresses ideas, thinks creatively, and organizes information in ways that are appropriate for grade one Comment or give examples: _In this sample, she wrote the Joseph Jacob's rendition of "The Three Little Pigs" from memory._		✓ 9/30	

IDEAS AND WORLD KNOWLEDGE	Not Yet	Some/Sometimes	All/Always
1-29. Demonstrates age appropriate world knowledge Comment or give examples: _Age appropriate for 9/30._		✓ 9/30	

ATTITUDES ABOUT READING AND WRITING	Not Yet	Some/Sometimes	All/Always
1-31. Chooses to write independently Comment or give examples: _Julie frequently chooses to write independently. With continued practice, she will develop more fully._		✓ 9/30	
1-33. Chooses to write in a sustained way for a period of time Comment or give examples: _Julie did this piece in one 45-minute writing workshop. She works persistently._		✓ 9/30	
1-35. Chooses writing related activities for enjoyment Comment or give examples:		✓ 9/30	

Julie's assessment demonstrates that writing and spelling provide concrete evidence of a child's position on the literacy map. Writing and spelling may be your most accessible evidence of what a child knows and your best clues for determining how to focus your instruction for that particular individual. **Step One** of the September Baseline Benchmark Check has allowed us to quickly and efficiently check Julie's progress on first-grade benchmark numbers 12, 14, 15, 16, 20, 21, 22, 23, 24, 25, 27, 28, 29, 31, 33, and 35. To complete the analysis, we proceed with **Step Two.**

STEP TWO: Some benchmarks cannot be assessed from the writing sample. Go through each remaining benchmark and consider each of the 10 essential literacy requirements. Assess the child's progress on the remaining benchmarks.

The remainder of Julie's benchmarks cannot be assessed from the writing sample. The next step would be to go through the remaining benchmarks considering each of the 10 essential literacy requirements and assess Julie's progress. Many of these remaining benchmarks would be assessed informally during the school day in whole class and guided group activity as well as in interviews with Julie in individual conferences. The following section provides assessment strategies and teaching activities for the 10 essential literacy requirements of first grade.

ASSESS LISTENING COMPREHENSION

Everyday reading/writing first-grade provides numerous opportunities for the teacher to observe and interview each child in order to assess listening comprehension. For example, you can assess after read-alouds and storytelling and during individual conferences. Children need experience and practice in retelling and responding to comprehension questions, but both should be modeled for students before these techniques are used for assessment (Glazer, 1992). Here are some informal ways of assessing comprehension:

- Observe children as they respond to the text.
- Talk with children about the material they read.
- Ask children to tell where the story happened.
- Ask children to describe one main character.
- Ask children to describe what happened in the story.

To assess comprehension more formally, you might keep anecdotal records to document information gained through observation and conversation. You might have children retell the story in sequence and tape-record or transcribe the retelling. The retelling could be analyzed to assess understanding of setting, character recall and development, events, and plot.

ASSESS EXPOSURE TO PRINT

A two-hour language arts block is *sine qua non* for successful teaching and literacy assessment. Consult the sample schedules in Chapter 3 as you think about how you might observationally assess children's literacy development in each of the essential literacy element areas. Remember, your best opportunity to collect assessment data occurs daily, in the classroom, as you work with children individually and observe them in groups and conferences.

Reread the first-grade benchmarks for Exposure to Print. The benchmarks assess if the child selects books at an appropriate level, reads independently in a sustained way for a period of time, reads at home and at school, and rereads books introduced in reading instruction. Each of these benchmarks can best be assessed observationally during the school day and in interviews with the child and parent. Noting what children are doing during individual reading time is one true test for assessing exposure to print. Expect children to spend about 20 minutes reading or rereading independently during the school day and about 20 minutes at home. A large volume of reading will bring gains in every essential literacy element area. Children who read become better writers and tend to improve as spellers. They also develop larger vocabularies, greater word specific knowledge, and knowledge in the content areas.

TEACHING ACTIVITY: MAXIMIZE EXPOSURE TO BOOKS

Too many children don't read because they have not been matched to books, guided, and adequately encouraged to read on their own. Maximize each child's exposure to books that are easy enough for the child to read. There is generally a range of five to eight levels of reading materials for first-grade. Match children to books at a level they can handle. At the beginning of the year, expect to match many of your first graders who are developmentally on track to books like *Run! Run!* or *"Pop" Pops the Popcorn*. Roughly five to eight levels and nine months later, you will be matching children to books like *Frog and Toad Are Friends* and *Amelia Bedelia* (examples of text to follow). If you use a basal, match children to the appropriate levels of those texts.

In addition to matching children to books, you must guide reading and establish a classroom in which children spend a lot of time reading independently. Your first graders will eventually learn to select books appropriate for their level of development on their own. They will learn to try the text and decide whether the book is "just right" for them—that is, just right to read and comprehend.

Imagine a first-grade classroom where children have access to lots of books and a knowledgeable teacher to help them select books that are interesting and easy for them to read. Each child has a book bag with at least five "just right" books for independent reading and rereading. In the back of the room there are five bins, color coded, filled with leveled text so that children can replace books read with new selections at their appropriate level.

In first grade, the easier texts have one to three lines of type on each page, very uniform structure, and strong picture clues. The harder texts, five to eight levels higher which children will be expected to read by the end of the year, include the first chapter books. These are more elaborate stories that extend over several pages and have unfamiliar and varied vocabulary, complex sentence structure, and few pictures to cue specific words in the text. Picture book folk tales may fall into the end of first-grade category, but unlike the picture books at the beginning of first grade, the primary purpose of the pictures in end of first-grade benchmark books is for aesthetic enhancement rather than cueing the reading. Notice the range in the samples of beginning versus end of first-grade texts presented on the next few pages.

TEXT FOR BEGINNING OF FIRST GRADE

Run! Run! by JoAnn Vandine
[Level C, *Guided Reading* Fountas and Pinnell, 1996]

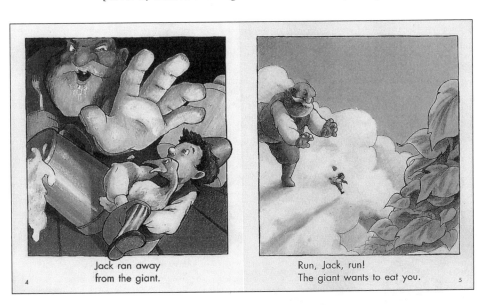

Jack ran away
from the giant.

Run, Jack, run!
The giant wants to eat you.

TEXT FOR BEGINNING OF FIRST GRADE

"Pop" Pops the Popcorn by Bob Egan
(Matches Fountas and Pinnell criteria for Level D.)

Get a box.
Get a mop.
The popcorn is popping over the top.

"POP" pops the popcorn.
When will it stop?

6   7

Greedy Cat Is Hungry by Joy Cowley
[Level D, *Guided Reading* Fountas and Pinnell, 1996]

Greedy Cat sat
on a mat
by the fridge.
Meow, meow, meow!

"No!" said Uncle.
"You're a greedy cat!"

6   7

Contrast these samples with the following two samples that readers who are developmentally on track might be reading by the end of first grade.

TEXT FOR END OF FIRST GRADE

Amelia Bedelia by Peggy Parish
[Level K, *Guided Reading* Fountas and Pinnell, 1996]

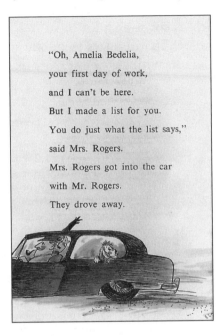

"Oh, Amelia Bedelia,
your first day of work,
and I can't be here.
But I made a list for you.
You do just what the list says,"
said Mrs. Rogers.
Mrs. Rogers got into the car
with Mr. Rogers.
They drove away.

Frog and Toad Are Friends by Arnold Lobel
[Level K, *Guided Reading,* Fountas and Pinnell, 1996]

A sparrow flew down.
"Excuse me," said the sparrow.
"Did you lose a button? I found one."
"That is not my button," said Toad.
"That button has two holes.
My button had four holes."
Toad put the button with two holes
in his pocket.

32

They went back to the woods
and looked on the dark paths.
"Here is your button," said Frog.
"That is not my button," cried Toad.
"That button is small.
My button was big."
Toad put the small button
in his pocket.

ASSESSMENT ACTIVITY: MATCHING CHILDREN WITH BOOKS

One of the most important jobs the first-grade teacher has is matching children to books. Studies have found that accuracy in reading words is much more important for first-grade comprehension than other factors related to reading, such as covering a lot of stories (Juel, 1994). In other words, it is better to match first-graders to books and give them practice reading text they can handle with very few errors than to cover all the stories in a basal reader.

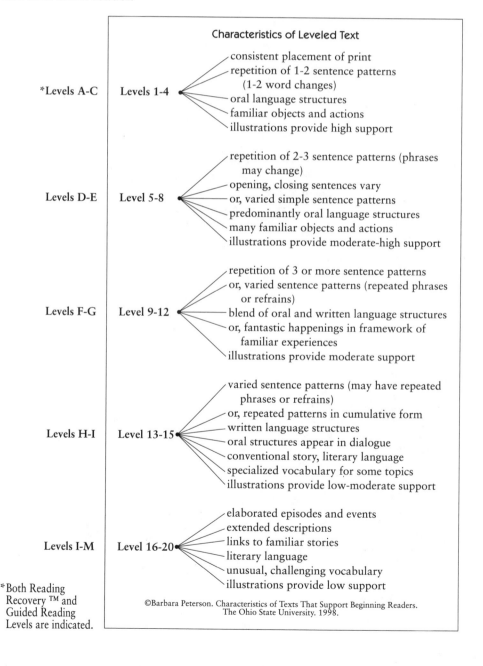

Characteristics of Leveled Text

*Levels A-C   Levels 1-4
- consistent placement of print
- repetition of 1-2 sentence patterns (1-2 word changes)
- oral language structures
- familiar objects and actions
- illustrations provide high support

Levels D-E   Level 5-8
- repetition of 2-3 sentence patterns (phrases may change)
- opening, closing sentences vary
- or, varied simple sentence patterns
- predominantly oral language structures
- many familiar objects and actions
- illustrations provide moderate-high support

Levels F-G   Level 9-12
- repetition of 3 or more sentence patterns
- or, varied sentence patterns (repeated phrases or refrains)
- blend of oral and written language structures
- or, fantastic happenings in framework of familiar experiences
- illustrations provide moderate support

Levels H-I   Level 13-15
- varied sentence patterns (may have repeated phrases or refrains)
- or, repeated patterns in cumulative form
- written language structures
- oral structures appear in dialogue
- conventional story, literary language
- specialized vocabulary for some topics
- illustrations provide low-moderate support

Levels I-M   Level 16-20
- elaborated episodes and events
- extended descriptions
- links to familiar stories
- literary language
- unusual, challenging vocabulary
- illustrations provide low support

*Both Reading Recovery ™ and Guided Reading Levels are indicated.

©Barbara Peterson. Characteristics of Texts That Support Beginning Readers. The Ohio State University. 1998.

Here are some basic guidelines for matching children to books. Select a range of books at different levels of difficulty. Have the child look through the books to find one that interests her or him and is not too hard and not too easy. The book should be "just right."

Have the child read a section of the book and ask, "How does that feel? Too hard, too easy, or just right?" In general, if the child is missing more than one in 10 words, the text will probably be too difficult, even for guided reading in which you are providing support. If the child has been well-matched to a book, he or she should be able to respond appropriately to the comprehension questions listed on the chart below. (Figure 5.2)

Selections for guided reading or "the reading group" should be on the level at which the reader needs a little support to handle the text. Generally, children grouped for guided reading should work with texts that they can read with about 90 to 95% accuracy.

MATCHING CHILDREN WITH BOOKS

When does the text match for independent reading?
Child reads independently with 95% to 100% accuracy.
Child accurately comprehends.
    Retells the story or content adequately or completely
    Responds appropriately to comprehension questions:
        Who are the characters?
        What is happening in the story?
        What is the problem?
        Where does the story take place?
        How did the story end?

(Remember, the higher the percentage of words that can be read, the higher the ultimate reading comprehension in first-grade.)

When does the text match for guided reading (instructional level)?
Child reads with 90% to 95% accuracy.
Child accurately comprehends with some guidance.
    Retells the story or context adequately
    Responds appropriately to comprehension questions
    Makes logical predictions
    Rereads independently after guided reading

When doesn't the text match?
Child recognizes 89% (or less) of the words accurately.
Child doesn't comprehend.
Child can't retell the story or context.

Figure 5.2

ASSESS READING COMPREHENSION

An end of year benchmark for first grade is that the child read aloud with fluency (as you take a running record—see page 47) and comprehend any text appropriately designed for the first half of grade one. Here are some examples:

TEXT FOR BEGINNING OF FIRST GRADE

Sheep in a Jeep by Nancy Shaw
[Level G, *Guided Reading,* Fountas and Pinnell, 1996]

TEXT FOR FIRST HALF OF FIRST GRADE

Goodnight Moon by Margaret Wise Brown
[Level H, *Guided Reading,* Fountas and Pinnell, 1996]

In the great green room
There was a telephone
And a red balloon
And a picture of—

The cow jumping over the moon

And there were three little bears sitting on chairs

By the end of first grade the child should read and comprehend both fiction and nonfiction comparable to *Frog and Toad Are Friends* (see page 73), *Amelia Bedelia* (see page 73), and *Dinosaurs* (shown on the next page), which fit the design for the second half of grade one. In reading these texts, the child should be able to predict and justify what will happen next. The child should be able to discuss "how," "who," and "what if" questions in nonfiction selections, and the child should self-correct using phonics, word specific knowledge, and semantic and syntactic cues.

TEXT FOR END OF FIRST GRADE

Dinosaurs by Michael Collins
(Level K, *Guided Reading,* Fountas and Pinnell, 1996)

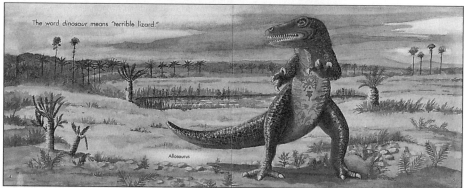

ASSESSMENT THROUGH RUNNING RECORDS

Running records, a technique developed by Marie Clay (1993), can be used to assess children's oral reading and comprehension. (For a complete description, see pages 47-49.) This procedure is an easy way to record which strategies a reader is using.

ASSESS PHONEMIC AWARENESS

First graders should demonstrate full phonemic awareness by midyear. The easiest way to assess this benchmark is to look at the child's invented spelling. Children who are Stage 3 (phonetic spellers) demonstrate full phonemic awareness because, by definition, Stage 3 spellers spell by ear and represent all the phonemes in the word. A child has to be *aware* of the phonemes to produce the phonetic spelling. Look at the phonetic spellings below. Each spelling represents all the phonemes in the spoken word.

WORD	DICTIONARY TRANSCRIPTION	PHONETIC SPELLING STAGE 3	EVIDENCE OF PHONEMIC AWARENESS
tooth	(tuth)	TUTH	All 3 phonemes represented.
fairy	(far-e)	FARE	All 4 phonemes represented.
eighty	(at-e)	ATE	All 3 phonemes represented.
you	(u)	U	1 of 1 phoneme represented.
bit	(bit)	BET	All 3 phonemes represented.
*Martian	(mar-sh n)	MRSHN	All 6 phonemes represented.
space	(spas)	SPAS	All 4 phonemes represented.

*Note: R-controlled vowel carries the vowel sound.
Syllabic *n* carries vowel in second syllable.

To assess phonemic awareness, I often use my simple invention called "The Camel Test." *Camel* is a word most first-graders have in their spoken vocabularies by midyear, but they are not likely to have seen *camel* often in print. In January, I ask the first-grader to spell *camel*. If the child says "C-A-M-L," she's likely to have phonemic awareness. (If the child has been exposed to the printed word *camel*, substitute a word such as eagle (EGL), bacon (BAKN), or magic (MAJEK).

An elaborated treatment of assessment, along with teaching activities for phonemic awareness, is presented under "Assess Phonemic Awareness" for kindergarten in Chapter 4. Consult Chapter 4 for additional assessment strategies and teaching activities.

ASSESS KNOWLEDGE OF REGULAR PHONICS PATTERNS

First-grade teachers must be aware of what each student knows about phonics and whether knowledge of regular phonics patterns is developing. What your students must learn is really quite basic: By midyear they should demonstrate that they are beginning to read regular c-v-c short vowel patterns (e.g., *pup, run, bib, web*) and words with combinations of consonant sounds (e.g., *milk, hand, nest, stamp*). They should recognize some high frequency, regular, long vowel patterns (e.g., v-c-e in *bake* and *bike*) and a few high frequency vowel combinations (e.g., *meat, need, boat*).

As a teacher, you should assess each child based on the expectations cited in the grade level benchmarks for regular phonics patterns. If the child doesn't have this knowledge, decide how best you can teach it.

> Avoid giving first-graders phonics instruction before they understand the alphabet principle or have the phonemic awareness necessary to learn regular phonics patterns.

A lack of phonemic awareness at the end of kindergarten severely limits a child's likelihood of learning regular phonics patterns in first-grade. When first-graders don't have the necessary insights about print at the beginning of the year, they are not likely to respond well to phonics instruction (Juel, 1994, p.125). There is also the problem of too much phonics instruction. It can be debilitating. The child ends up concentrating so intently on sounding out and blending that reading to get the meaning or the fluency of real reading isn't possible. We have all seen children who could decode text but not understand a word of what they were reading.

THE TIMING OF PHONICS INSTRUCTION

There is a relatively short time when direct phonics instruction for the purpose of teaching children to read makes sense. That time comes in the first half of first-grade when children need to be showing evidence that they are developing knowledge of regular phonics patterns. By January of the first-grade year, children should be accurately decoding some phonetically regular, one syllable words with the c-v-c (*bat, run*) and v-c-e (*cake, late*) patterns. They should be able to read pseudowords such as *dit, buf,* and *yode,* and they should be using this knowledge to sound out unknown words when reading text. They should be using some regular c-v-c and v-c-e patterns in their invented spelling. If most of your first-grade students aren't doing this, you need to focus more on phonics instruction.

Research shows that first graders who are not developing knowledge of regular phonics patterns by the middle of first grade need intervention.

These children "are almost invariably poor readers at the end of first grade". If a child doesn't demonstrate this kind of knowledge in January, I am in agreement with research that suggests instructional intervention is essential. (Juel, 1994, p. 125).

TYPES OF PHONICS INSTRUCTIONS

It is generally agreed that phonics must be taught. The issues concern *when*, as discussed above, and *how*. Different approaches often have much in common as demonstrated in the following chart.

Part-to-Whole Instruction	Whole-to-Part Instruction
Occurs before reading and is built from letters to words.	Occurs after text has been read to, with, and by children and starts with whole text, then goes to words and to word parts.
Systematic: High frequency regular phonics patterns are presented sequentially, proceeding from simple to more complex.	**Systematic:** High frequency regular phonics patterns are presented sequentially, proceeding from simple to more complex.
Intensive: Up to 20 minutes of classroom time is focused on teaching all high frequency letter-sound correspondences at the start of reading.	**Extensive:** Time spent after reading is focused on teaching high frequency letter-sound correspondences until children understand the concept and can generalize to other letter-sound correspondences at the same level of complexity. Then they move to the next level of complexity.
Explicit: Each high frequency letter-sound correspondence is taught directly.	**Strategic:** Based on assessed needs, high frequency letter-sound correspondences are taught directly.

The following information is relevant, no matter how you approach phonics instruction. It is good, for example, for first graders to know roughly 49 high frequency letter-sound correspondences.

As you consider this section, keep in mind that children should be properly prepared for phonics instruction. Instruction in kindergarten should be designed to provide full and adequate preparation, including knowledge of the alphabet and phonemic awareness. If you have questions about what your first graders should know before you plot your phonics instruction, review the kindergarten benchmarks in Chapter 4.

HIGH FREQUENCY LETTER-SOUND CORRESPONDENCES

First-graders should learn the following:

a	as in *bat*	l		v	
m		o	as in *hot*	e	as in *bed*
t		h		u-e	as in *use*
s		u	as in *cup*	p	
i	as in *sit*	c	as in *cap*	w	as in *wet*
f		b		j	
a-e	as in *cake*	n		i-e	as in *like*
d		k		y	as in *yoke*
r		o-e	as in *home*	z	
g	as in *goat*				

Once learned, focus on more complex letter-sound correspondences:

ch	as in *chip*	ou	as in *cloud*	kn	as in *knot*
ea	as in *meat*	oy	as in *boy*	oa	as in *boat*
ee	as in *need*	ph	as in *phone*	oi	as in *boil*
er	as in *her*	qu	as in *quick*	ai	as in *maid*
ay	as in *day*	sh	as in *ship*	ar	as in *car*
igh	as in *high*	th	as in *thank*	au	as in *haul*
ew	as in *new*	ir	as in *girl*	aw	as in *paw*

Burmeister (1975) identified a set of approximately 45 letter-sound correspondences that have a utility rate high enough to justify instruction. Many phonics advocates recommend presentation of patterns like the ones listed above in a structured sequence (Carnine, 1980).

Teach phonics through exposure to onsets and rimes.

What are onsets and rimes? An onset is the part of sound or the spelling pattern that comes before the first vowel in a word or syllable (/m/ in *mind*). A rime is the first vowel in a syllable and whatever follows (/ind/ in *mind*).

Onsets and rimes actually are sounds that can be represented by visual spelling patterns.

Word	Onset	Rime
big	b	-ig
sprig	spr	-ig
fling	fl	-ing
sing	s	-ing

Onsets and rimes are important because they are the most psychologically accessible units of sound that may be mapped to a spelling pattern (Goswami, 1996, p.5) Blending an onset with a rhyme requires children to put together two discrete sounds to form a recognizable word. About 500 easy to read, high frequency words can be derived from only 37 rimes (Wylie and Durrell, 1970). It may be important to teach the onsets and rimes because of their utility for spelling analogies (Cunningham, 1994).

-ack	-an	-aw	-ice	-in	-ir	-ore
-ain	-ank	-ay	-ick	-ine	-ock	-uck
-ake	-ap	-eat	-ide	-ing	-oke	-ug
-ale	-ash	-ell	-ight	-ink	-op	-ump
-all	-at	-est	-ill	-ip	-or	-unk
-ame	-ate					

Basic Guidelines for Teaching Phonics With Onsets and Rimes

- Have children listen for rime.
- Teach children to manipulate and to blend the onset to the rime.
- Teach onset and rime analogies, such as *n -et, j-et, p-et*.
- Chunk units such as *str-, ch-,* and *-ight* into one spelling pattern rather than sounding them out letter-by-letter.

Note: Patterns such as *-ight* are considered "irregular" and present problems if the child tries to blend each letter (i-g-h-t) into a sound. As a chunk, however, *-ight* is very consistent. If the sound in the rime *-ight* is matched to the spelling pattern *-ight*, it is very "regular" and is found in over 90 English words including *right, night, bright, flight, tight, light,* etc. (Goswami, 1996, p. 125).

- Teach spelling patterns that reflect rimes.

  N, E, and T spell net.
  Watch me spell net.
  n -et
  Name the two parts.
  N *represents the /n/ sound, and*
  ET *represents the /et/ sound.*

- Demonstrate how to blend the onset to the rime.

  Practice reading these words
  n -et
  g -et
  l -et
  b -et
  s -et
  j -et

- Teach children to use reading analogies by using a word they already know to try to read new words.

  If you can read net, *you can read* get, let, bet, set, jet.

- In second grade, practice with words of more than one syllable (*market, better*).
- Teach children to use spelling analogies by using a word they already know to try to spell new words.
- Group words according to the spelling of their rimes.

n -et	b -at
g -et	f -at
l -et	c -at
b -et	fl -at
s -et	s -at
j -et	spl -at

- After children master c-v-c and c-v-e patterns, introduce more complex rime families.

c-vcc	cc-vcc
t-ell	bl-ack
b-ell	sl-ack
w-ell	sm-ack
s-ell	tr-ack
f-ell	st-ack

- Have children practice spelling words in the same pattern families.
- Teach children explicitly to make analogies between shared spelling patterns and words because shared sounds can predict shared spellings.
- Teach double and triple letter onsets explicitly (*st-, str-, ch-*).

Basic Guidelines for Phonics Instruction

Phonics should be covered systematically, following a scope and sequence, and instruction should show how phonics applies to reading and writing. Initial lessons teach students that words consist of patterns of sounds and letters. Children learn how letters of the alphabet and chunks of letters, like the spelling patterns for onsets and rimes, correspond to sounds in words. Learning progresses from short vowel (c-v-c) patterns to silent *e* (c-v-e) patterns.

The focus in first grade should be on high-utility regular patterns which are mastered before increasingly difficult letter-sound correspondences are introduced (see page 82). While children may be exposed to many different patterns in their reading of books, do not focus on low-utility patterns, such as *-ey* and *-ough*, until students have mastered the most common patterns. (I address the low-utility patterns, beginning primarily with the second-grade benchmarks for specific word knowledge and spelling on page 125.) By the end of first-grade, students should be able to decode and blend many regular letter-sound correspondences, decode and blend patterns representing syllables or pseudowords (e.g., *dit, nuv, but*), and use phonics knowledge to sound out unknown words when reading text.

GENERAL SEQUENCE FOR PHONICS INSTRUCTION

- Phonemic awareness
- Letter recognition
- Letter-sound correspondences
- Chunks of letters/patterns, like onsets and rimes
- Common consonants
- Short vowels
- Silent *e* pattern
- Increasingly more difficult patterns

PART-TO-WHOLE: HIGH UTILITY PATTERNS

Activity 1. Learning Letter-Sound Correspondences

Initially lessons may introduce four or five common consonants and one or two short vowels that can be blended together to make phonetically regular, high-frequency words in the c-v-c pattern. These lessons teach children to create an orthographic system of matching one letter to one sound.

Start by saying the sound in isolation, then show the letter that represents the sound. Children repeat the sound and letter and practice naming objects beginning with the target sound. Key word pictures, showing objects with names that start with the target sound, can be introduced. The intent is to have children connect the sound to the letter.

Activity 2. Modeling and Applying: Blending

When the sounds of four or five consonants and a short vowel have been learned, place letter tiles or letter cards together in left-to-right sequence to form a word. (The word can also be written on a chart.) As you point to each letter, elongate each sound and blend the sounds together into a recognizable word. Repeat the process faster and more smoothly with children repeating the blending process with you—mapping sounds (i.e., phonemes) to letters in unison—until children blend the phonemes into a recognizable word.

Activity 3. Modeling and Applying: Reading the Words

Children practice reading various words with the c-v-c sequence. As soon as possible, they practice reading text to show them how phonics applies to reading.

Activity 4. Modeling and Applying: Writing the Words

Children practice writing and spelling phonetically regular, one syllable c-v-c words. They may copy the practice words into individual "sound books" or make word cards to take home for practice.

WHOLE-TO-PART: HIGH UTILITY PATTERNS

For whole class and/or small group sound and letter or spelling pattern explorations, first identify a target letter or sound based on an assessment of children's needs. Then find one or more texts containing the target letter or sound. Children should be familiar with the text(s) from previous encounters in shared reading.

Activity 1. Sound Exploration

The purpose is for children to understand that sounds can be represented by a variety of letter and letter combinations.

1. Read the text to children during or after shared reading.
2. Have children *listen* for a target sound.
3. As children identify words, list them on chart paper. Say each word and ask children to listen for the sound; underline the letter(s) that represent the sound in each word.
4. Sort the words according to the letter(s) that represent the sound.
5. Once the words are sorted, lead children to generalize about the different positions in which the letter(s) appeared and which letter(s) occurred most frequently.
6. Review the generalizations.

Activity 2. Letter or Spelling Pattern Exploration

The purpose is for children to understand that most letters represent more than one sound and to identify letters in all positions. The sequence for this exploration is the same as for a sound exploration.

1. Have children read the text along with you during shared reading.
2. Ask children to *look* for a target letter or spelling pattern. Remind them to look for the letter or pattern in all positions.
3. List the words on chart paper as the children identify them.
4. Sort the words according to the position of the letter or the various sounds the letter or spelling pattern represents.
5. Form generalizations.
6. Review generalizations.

WHERE DO YOUR FIRST GRADERS GO FROM HERE?

In second grade, children are taught to look for syllable units and practice decoding polysyllabic words. They accurately decode phonetically regular, two-syllable words and two-syllable pseudowords (such as *cosnuv* and *uncabe*). By the end of second grade, knowledge of common letter-sound correspondences for two and three-syllable words enable skilled readers to read polysyllabic words relatively effortlessly (Shefelbine, 1995. p. 4).

Remember, high frequency regular patterns should be mastered in first-grade. Many of the rarely occurring patterns are taught in second and third grade spelling lessons. (See also second and third-grade benchmarks for specific word knowledge). You must assess and be accountable for children's knowledge of regular phonics patterns. How you decide to teach phonics is your choice within the parameters of your local district mandates.

ASSESS WORD SPECIFIC KNOWLEDGE

By the end of first grade, children should have a reading vocabulary of words they recognize on sight of more than 100 high frequency words. They should recognize many common irregularly spelled words such as *have, said, where,* and *two,* and they should spell many first-grade-level spelling words, such as *the, at, bed, cut, five,* and *green,* correctly. The best way to teach vocabulary is through wide reading. The best way to assess word specific knowledge is to pay attention to what children do with words when they read and spell.

Assess word specific knowledge every time you listen to a child read aloud. The level of text a child can read independently provides a concrete measure of a first-grader's level of sight word recognition. Any child who can read *Frog and Toad Are Friends* (see page 73), for example, demonstrates very good first-grade-level word specific knowledge. A child who struggles to recognize words in *Run! Run!* (see page 71) does not have a stable sight vocabulary. While I believe it is best to assess word recognition through ongoing classroom observation in guided reading and through observation of independent reading, sometimes it is good to do a quick informal word recognition check to corroborate your observations. This may be conducted with word lists or with word walls as described below.

A QUICK, INFORMAL WORD RECOGNITION TEST

Reading teachers are familiar with informal reading inventories which provide grade level word lists for checking recognition of words in isolation. This test is one measure of word specific knowledge. In a variation of this test, a list of high frequency words appropriate for first-grade is presented on word cards or in list form (see pages 160-161). Ask the child to read aloud the words in the list he or she knows. Indicate recognized words with a check or by sorting recognized word cards in one stack. This quick, informal assessment will indicate if the child recognized virtually no words, some words, or many words. This is the basic information you need to determine whether word recognition is proceeding well or whether it needs more attention.

TEACHING ACTIVITY: WORD WALLS

Conventional wisdom has always supported the teaching of sight words for children who are learning to read in first grade. A popular and very good way to teach word specific knowledge in first-grade classrooms is the word wall. I recommend a word wall for every first-grade classroom, because it's such an effective way to teach word specific knowledge to beginning readers. The word wall is actually a big classroom dictionary that grows as new words are added each week.

To make a word wall, select a wall in the classroom on which you can display the letters of the alphabet in alphabetical order with space below each letter for displaying high frequency words that begin with that letter. The word wall needs to be on a wall, as opposed to a chart or bulletin board, so that it's large enough for each child to see the words from any location in the room.

Each week, five new high frequency sight words, taken from words children are currently encountering in their writing and reading, are added to the word wall for word specific study. Once a word is added to the wall, it stays up all year so children can use and practice it. By the end of the school year, most word walls will have grown to about 150 words.

The intent is that, through practice, each child will learn to recognize the words automatically. Many children will also learn to spell the high frequency words correctly. When writing, children may refer to the word wall for spelling help just as they would a dictionary.

Each day the teacher conducts a word wall practice lesson usually as a whole class activity for about ten minutes. Typically five or six words are practiced. The teacher notes which words children are using and having difficulty with in reading, writing, and spelling and those words are practiced in the ten minute word wall practice lessons each day.

SELECTING AND DISPLAYING WORD WALL WORDS

Word wall words should always consist of high frequency words that children use daily. The 100 frequently used words on page 56 are excellent word wall words. *Valentine* would not be a good word wall word because basically it's only used in February. (Words like *Valentine* are often highlighted at appropriate times on wall charts.) Teachers may also include easily confused words, such as *were, where, went,* and *want.* These words are generally added to the word wall one at a time to minimize confusion.

Words are displayed alphabetically by first letter. Teachers often display the words on pastel color cards, making sure to use different colors as a point of reference for easily confused words. For example, if seven words beginning with *w* are displayed on the wall, the teacher might say "*With* is the orange word" (on the orange card) to make sure children are looking at the appropriate word.

INTRODUCING A WORD WALL

Following is a basic procedure for introducing a word wall word:

1. Pronounce the word distinctly.
2. Present the word in context. High frequency words are in every-

thing—children's speech, their writing, in texts being read aloud, and in reading texts. I try to present the words in a context with which children are familiar. For example, if *very* is being introduced as a new word, I might refer to the story of *The Three Little Pigs* for context: "Today we're going to learn a new word wall word. The word is *very*." (hold up a colored card displaying the printed word *very*.) "The third little pig was very smart! Very."

3. Have children say the word and clap and chant the spelling. The clapping, chanting, and spelling routine can be used when new words are presented and when words are practiced. It's a multimodal strategy that's easy to follow and many first-grade teachers say it works, so I endorse it.

PRACTICING WORD WALL WORDS

It's helpful to vary word wall practice lessons. Pat Cunningham, who has written extensively about word walls, recommends five strategies that I find particularly useful (1994).

Write, Clap, and Chant fits nicely into 10 minutes of shared reading time during the reading workshop. The teacher calls out a word from the wall. Children write the word, then everyone pronounces the word and claps and chants the spelling to check what they have written. Sometimes instead of clapping I have children put a dot under each letter as that letter is called out in the chanting of the spelling.

Letter and Rhyme also takes about 10 minutes during shared reading time. The teacher calls out a word as follows: "The word rhymes with *fig* and begins with *p*." After children write the word, they pronounce the word in unison and clap and chant the spelling.

What Word Makes Sense is one of my favorites. The teacher prepares five sentence strips using the cloze procedure to highlight the target word (e.g., Little pig, little pig, _____ me come in!). A cue is given as to the beginning letter of the word. For example, the teacher writes *l* on the board and says "The first word begins with *l* and fits in the sentence: "Little pig, little pig, _____ me come in!" Children find *l* on the word wall and decide which word best fits in the sentence. They write the word (let), then everyone claps and chants the spelling. The sentence strip goes into a collection along with other strips already introduced in a literacy center where individuals or groups of two or three children may practice them later.

This is very valuable activity for shared reading that enables the teacher to model fluent reading and the voice to print match. She might use this activity to model the use of semantic and syntactic cues as a strategy for figuring out unknown words.

Word Wall Sentences is good for 10 minutes of shared writing during a writing workshop. By November, about 45 words should have been collected on the word wall, enough to allow the teacher to dictate a sentence such as "This little pig went home." After dictating the sentence, the teacher dictates each word again and allows time for children to write it. Then the teacher reminds children to start the sentence with a capital letter and end it with a period, thus, two important first-grade benchmarks for writing are addressed.

In **Read My Mind** children number a sheet of paper from one to five. The teacher selects a secret word from the word wall and writes it on a folded sheet of paper so that the word cannot be seen. Each time she gives a clue, children try to guess the secret word and write it on the paper. By the fifth clue, everyone should have guessed the word. Read My Mind is a fun way to practice writing and spelling word wall words, but it also may be used to highlight any metacognitive concepts such as beginning letters and vowels.

(For more information on word walls, see Cunningham, Pat, *Phonics They Use*. New York: HarperCollins, 1995.)

To check on children's learning of words, have two children work together using the following procedure:

> The first child asks the second child to write each of the words the second child has been learning during the week. (If the first child is not sure how to say one of the words the second child can help.)
> The children swap tasks.

> Each child then checks his spelling with the original list. If a word is incorrect, it may be added to the list for the next week.

ASSESS SPELLING DEVELOPMENT

Spelling—Snapshots of the First-Grade Mind

Spelling provides a concrete picture of many of the first-grade essential literacy elements. You can literally "see" phonemic awareness by looking at what a child does with spelling. You can "see" phonics development. You can "see" development of word specific knowledge, aspects of writing, and even reading development by looking at spelling. In first grade, *spelling is a tool for knowing children individually and tracking their journey on the literacy map.*

Invented and correct spelling help you assess phonemic awareness, knowledge of regular phonics, word specific knowledge, and spelling.

Remember our first-grader, Julie, who wrote her own version of "The Three Little Pigs"? (Chapter 2, page 15) Figure 5.3 shows how spelling provided a concrete picture—a snapshot into Julie's mind—that shows what she knew and helped to pinpoint where she was on the first-grade literacy map in four essential literacy element areas.

SOME SNAPSHOTS OF JULIE'S LITERACY DEVELOPMENT

Julie's Spelling	Essential Element	What It Shows
BUNDL for *bundle* LITL for *little* MUTHR for *mother*	Phonemic Awareness	Julie's awareness of the number of syllables in words is demonstrated when she spells these two-syllable words phonetically (Benchmark 1-12).
67% Phonetic Spelling	Phonemic Awareness Spelling	Julie is a Stage 3 speller. By definition, Stage 3 spellers demonstrate full phonemic awareness (Benchmark 1-14).
GIV for *give* SED for *said* BILD for *build* UV for *of*	Knowledge of Regular Phonics	Julie reads back her own writing and accurately decodes *pig, met* and *man*, demonstrating ability to decode some regular, one-syllable patterns in her own writing (Benchmark 1-15). In some words Julie attempted, correct spelling is irregular, but Julie demonstrates that she knows a regular phonic spelling for the sound of the word. She accurately decodes phonic spellings such as GIV and SED when she reads her writing.

Julie's Spelling	Essential Element	What It Shows
BUN in *bundle* LIT in *little* MUTH in *mother*	Knowledge of Regular Phonics	Julie accurately decodes nonsense word parts *bun, lit,* and *muth* in her own writing (Benchmark 1-16). *Bun, lit,* and *muth,* not words in Julie's speaking vocabulary, might function as fragments, i.e., if she can spell the syllable *muth* she can spell the nonsense fragment *muth*.
one, a, pig, sent, her, met, with, me, my	Word Specific Knowledge	Julie spells a collection of first-grade-level words (Benchmark 1-20).
67% Phonetic Spelling	Spelling	Julie matches all of the sounds in words with an appropriate letter correspondence (Benchmark 1-23).
22% Transitional Spelling	Spelling	Julie is not yet a Stage 4, Transitional Speller (Benchmark 1-24). She doesn't represent many of the visual conventions of English spelling, such as vowels in every syllable.
pig, met, man, sent	Spelling	Julie correctly spells some three and four letter phonetically regular, short vowel words, but she lacks consistency with this important pattern (Benchmark 1-25).
one	Spelling	Julie correctly spells a few high frequency, irregular sight words. (Benchmark 1-27).

Figure 5.3

The Gentry Developmental Spelling Test

Many teachers and school districts have found The Gentry Developmental Spelling Test to be an important tool for first-grade assessment. This quick and efficient way to assess developmental spelling, first published in *Teaching K-8* (Gentry, 1985), is fully described in *Teaching Kids to Spell,* (Gentry and Gillet, 1993, pages 39-48).

Each invented spelling is a permanent record of an individual's journey to spelling competence. If we collect these snapshots, these invented spellings, and analyze them, we can put together a remarkable album that shows milestones along the way. Since the journey unfolds developmentally in patterns that are predictable and systematic, we can chart the journey with precision and accuracy.

The Gentry Developmental Spelling Test pinpoints a child's developmental spelling progress on the literacy map by helping teachers recognize the qualitative changes children make in how they invent spellings.

Teachers use this test to determine the child's stage of development at a particular time—essentially to map the child's journey with spelling development. The journey goes through the following stages:

Stage 1	Stage 2	Stage 3	Stage 4	Stage 5
Precommunicative	Semiphonetic	Phonetic	Transitional	Conventional
Random Letters	Abbreviated Spelling	Spelling by Ear	Spelling by Eye	Correct Spelling
Kindergarten	Kindergarten	first-grade	first-grade	Grades
Benchmark K-22	Benchmark K-23	Benchmark 1-23	Benchmark 1-24	Two-Eight

One of the attractive features of this test is that it is short and can be administered to the whole class at one time. The test is easily scored via a description of each developmental level and a simple scoring chart. Unlike most spelling tests, this one is not merely concerned with whether the word is correct or incorrect, but with a more finely tuned assessment of where the child fits on the developmental scale. After teachers use The Gentry Developmental Spelling Test a few times, they become adept at recognizing the five developmental levels, and they can easily analyze developmental spelling in a child's writing and pinpoint the writer's level of spelling development.

When administering this test, make sure children know that they are not supposed to know the dictionary spellings of these words yet. Sometimes I introduce the test this way: "Today we're going to take a spelling test just like older children. I want you to do your best, but don't worry if you do not know the correct spelling of some of the words. This test will show me how you think when you try to spell third, fourth, or fifth grade level spelling words. It will not be graded as right or wrong. You aren't supposed to know the dictionary spelling of all these words yet."

THE GENTRY DEVELOPMENTAL SPELLING TEST
(The "Monster" Test)

Call out each of the following words. Use each word in a sentence and say the word again.

1. monster
2. united
3. dress
4. bottom
5. hiked

6. human
7. eagle
8. closed
9. bumped
10. typed

[These words were selected because they represent specific aspects of phonetic form such as preconsonantal nasals, intervocalic flaps, and affricates—phonetic forms that children systematically spell in different ways at different levels of development. For a full explanation of the five levels of developmental spelling and a more technical treatment of the sound features represented in children's invented spelling see, *Teaching Kids to Spell,* (Gentry and Gillet, 1993, pp. 21-37).]

Analyze Each Spelling

1. Look at the child's spelling of each word. Find the type of error in the scoring chart (Figure 5.4) that best matches the child's spelling. If no match is found, consult the stage descriptions to determine a match (Figure 5.5).

2. Designate the appropriate developmental level beside each of the 10 words. Use Pre or 1 for precommunicative (Stage 1); SP or 2 for semiphonetic (Stage 2); P or 3 for phonetic (Stage 3); T or 4 for transitional (Stage 4); and C or 5 for conventional (Stage 5).

3. Count the number of spellings at each stage. The child's probable stage is the level most frequently used on this test. A majority of the spellings usually fall into one category. Verify the test findings by noting which stage you see the child using in invented spelling in authentic writing.

SCORING CHART

Stage 1 Precommunicative	Stage 2 Semiphonetic	Stage 3 Phonetic	Stage 4 Transitional	Stage 5 Conventional
1. random letters	mtr	mostr	monstur	monster
2. random	u	unitd	younighted	united
3. random	jrs	jras	dres	dress
4. random	bt	bodm	bottum	bottom
5. random	h	hikt	hicked	hiked
6. random	um	humn	humun	human
7. random	eg	ehl	egul	eagle
8. random	kid	klosd	clossed	closed
9. random	bt	bopt	bumpped	bumped
10. random	tp	tip	tipe	type

Figure 5.4

STAGE DESCRIPTIONS

Stage 1, Precommunicative Spelling: The word is spelled with random letters.

Stage 2, Semiphonetic Spelling: The spelling is an abbreviated phonetic spelling. Some of the phonemes in the word are not represented in this spelling. These are often one, two, or three letter spellings; however, occasionally random letters are added to the abbreviated semiphonetic spelling. Both JRS and JlRPPS would be semiphonetic spellings for *dress*.

Stage 3, Phonetic Spelling: The word is spelled "by ear" with all the sounds represented. The words may not look like English spelling (e.g., EGL for *eagle*, UNITID for *united*). The preconsonantal nasal sound is spelled by leaving out N or M before a consonant (MOSTR for *monster*); otherwise, you will see a phonetically appropriate letter representing each sound in the word.

Stage 4, Transitional Spelling: The word is spelled "by eye," that is, it looks like English spelling. Visual conventions of English spelling are apparent such as vowels in every syllable, common English letter sequences, vowel digraphs, the silent *e* marking the long vowel, and the endings *-s, -ed,* and *-ing* being spelled conventionally. Sometimes the word is correctly spelled except for transposition of some of the letters in the correct spelling (e.g., OPNE for *open*, HUOSE for *house*).

Stage 5, Conventional Spelling: The word is spelled correctly.

Note: If a two-syllable word is spelled with one syllable in one stage and one syllable in another stage, rank the word at the lower stage. For example, if *monster* (mon-ster)is spelled MOSTUR, the first syllable is phonetic due to the treatment of the preconsonantal nasal as explained in Stage 3 above. But the second syllable is transitional because STUR represents all the sounds in the syllable *ster*, and it looks like an acceptable English spelling. While MOSTUR is actually MO (phonetic) plus STUR (transitional), rank the word at the lower level. Thus MOSTUR is a Stage 3, phonetic spelling.

Figure 5.5

Following is a sample Scoring Sheet. See page 159 for a reproducible Spelling Test Scoring Sheet.

THE GENTRY DEVELOPMENTAL SCORING SHEET
For Two Administrations

	STAGE			STAGE
1. mostr	P		1. monstur	t
2. unitd	P		2. younihted	t
3. dras	P		3. dres	t
4. botm	P		4. botum	t
5. hict	P		5. hicked	t
6. hmn	sp		6. humn	P
7. egl	P		7. egul	t
8. kls	sp		8. clossed	t
9. bumt	P		9. bumt	P
10. tip	P		10. tipe	t

Name Bill
Date Nov. 15
Stage Phonetic
 semi 20%
 Phonetic 80%

Name Bill
Date Feb. 15
Stage transitional
 Phonetic 20%
 transitional 80%

ASSESS WRITING

The first-grade writing benchmarks assure that by the end of first grade a child should be able to produce a variety of short compositions, and use basic punctuation and capitalization. The first-grade year will not produce a Tolstoy or a Shakespeare. Many years of experience reading and listening to stories read aloud help developing writers learn the conventions writers use to shape a composition and communicate effectively.

As the teacher, you should spend a lot of time practicing and developing a basic foundation for writing in first grade. Model production of different types of short compositions, basic punctuation, and capitalization. Show children when what they write makes sense and when it's confusing to the reader, and show them how to fix it.

The samples below and on the next page show how Quonicus's first-grade writing changed over time. His progress demonstrates what it looks like to be on track for meeting the minimal acceptable criteria for what should be happening in first-grade from the beginning to the end of the year.

Figure 5.6

Figure 5.6 is a sample written on September 10. While Quonicus, at this time a Stage 2 semiphonetic speller, has met the end-of-kindergarten benchmarks, he clearly has not yet met the first-grade-writing benchmarks. He hasn't had enough experience writing to meet benchmark 1-21. He uses mostly capital letters, and his concept of periods is to place one at the end of each line. Clearly, he hasn't met benchmark 1-22.

WRITING	Not Yet	Some/Sometimes	Good Variety
1-21. Produces a variety of short compositions (e.g., stories, simple descriptions, journal entries)	✓ 9/10		

1-22. Uses basic punctuation and capitalization	Not Yet	Some/Sometimes	All/Always
	✓ 9/10		

Figure 5.7

Figure 5.8

Quonicus's November samples (Figures 5.10 and 5.11) show progress. He's writing longer compositions that show some variation in format. He shows development in his use of periods and capitalizes the first word of each sentence. He has advanced to "sometimes" for both writing benchmarks.

WRITING	Not Yet	Some/Sometimes	Good Variety
1-21. Produces a variety of short compositions (e.g., stories, simple descriptions, journal entries)	✓ 9/10	✓ 11/24	

1-22. Uses basic punctuation and capitalization	Not Yet	Some/Sometimes	All/Always
	✓ 9/10	✓ 11/24 2/4	

Figure 5.9

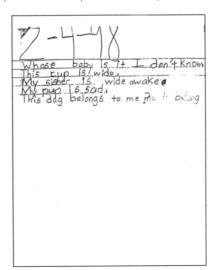

Figure 5.10

The January/February benchmark check shows that Quonicus is on track for successfully achieving the writing benchmarks for first-grade, but he hasn't made it yet. In fact, he hasn't progressed a great deal since November. By the end of the year his compositions should be longer and show more variety. He has introduced dialogue in Figure 5.9, a positive sign that he is adding variety to his compositions. He doesn't know about quotation marks. Of more concern is his omission of some punctuation in Figure 5.9 and his lack of consistency with questions marks in Figure 5.10. Based on what he was doing in November, one would have expected more stable punctuation. The need for additional help with punctuation in the ensuing months is clearly indicated.

Quonicus is doing a fairly good job with capitalization. Modeling more variety in composition and showing him how to develop lengthier, more substantial compositions would be appropriate goals between February and the end of first grade. He needs to begin to pay more attention to editing and revision and to making sure his writing makes sense. For example, he leaves out words in Figure 5.9. He writes *It Satruday*, for *It is Saturday*. He leaves the reader wondering what *the boy had a leggtleg* means. "Does this say, 'The boy had a little league game?'" I would ask him. If it does I would ask why that sentence pops up in the middle of a story called "Feed the Puppy." I might say "Quonicus, tell me more about the little league game. Why is it important to mention the little league game in a story about feeding the puppy?"

I notice in the illustration Quonicus has added some detail to the boy's right leg. Is the sentence not about a little league game but about a broken leg? I would bring up this issue with Quonicus and talk about editing the piece to make sure the reader gets Quonicus's intended meaning. "Quonicus, I'm not sure I know what this says. Read it for me." Our discussions would go from there. I might nudge Quonicus to write more on the topic of feeding the puppy and show him how to edit by putting in words he left out. He might have another go at the *leggtleg* spelling after we discuss it. Maybe we would look it up or I might just give him the correct spelling. Our discussion about his piece would allow me to make intuitive decisions about which issues—spelling, omitting words, making sense, revision, sticking to the topic—need focus.

The midyear assessment shows that Quonicus needs more time for writing. Effective writing needs to be modeled for Quonicus so he can see how his current work can improve. As a teacher, I might decide to interact more with Quonicus individually in roving conferences. I would raise the level of expectations, but let him be fully aware that I know he can meet or surpass the writing benchmarks by the end of his first-grade year.

First graders should be writing 45 minutes a day in the context of a writing workshop. The teacher begins the year with a great deal of modeled writing, giving way to shared writing, and finally to much more independent writing as individuals gain more control. Students like Quonicus who are placed in this kind of context meet the writing benchmarks.

ASSESS IDEAS AND WORLD KNOWLEDGE

"Ideas and World Knowledge" refers to whether the child expresses ideas, thinks creatively, organizes information appropriate for first-grade, and demonstrates "appropriate world knowledge." I think this essential element is best assessed informally through observation. In my view, teachers who live within a community of learners in a reading/writing classroom get to know each student well enough to assess these benchmarks. Those who put more emphasis on cultural literacy may prefer more rigorous standards for assessment, such as E. D. Hirsch's, *What Your First (also Second and Third) Grader Needs to Know* (1991).

Throughout this book, my emphasis is on excellent basic education in reading, writing, and spelling. It is my experience that the best way to meet the Ideas and World Knowledge benchmarks is to establish a first-grade classroom where children have access to books and spend time reading and writing.

ASSESS ATTITUDES ABOUT READING AND WRITING

The central question in an assessment of "Attitudes About Reading and Writing" is whether the child engages in stimulating and active performance in these areas. Teachers have no difficulty assessing these benchmarks when they know their students, make school useful and interesting, create reading/writing classrooms, and personalize instruction.

I prefer observational assessment of attitudes. Notice that this is the only essential literacy element that repeats the same benchmark questions year after year. Other benchmarks such as those for Phonics Knowledge, Spelling, or Writing change qualitatively each year. In most essential element areas, you "raise the bar" or assess for a higher level of performance each year. You never really "raise the bar" when assessing attitudes. It's not the standards that change when assessing attitudes—it's the child's attitude that might change. A child who had good attitudes about reading and writing in kindergarten may have developed poor ones in first-grade. Children who had great attitudes in second grade may need new motivation in third grade. You can assess that change by asking the same attitude questions you asked in kindergarten. How you ask the questions and how children respond, of course, becomes more sophisticated as children mature.

Chapter 5 has enabled you to determine if each of your students has successfully negotiated the first-grade literacy map. Know each first-grader individually and provide intervention for children who may not be successfully reaching the end of first-grade benchmarks. Remember, nine out of 10 children who are poor readers at the end of first grade continue to be poor readers (Juel, 1994). First grade may be the most important year in a child's journey to literacy. It's imperative that children successfully negotiate the first-grade literacy map.

CHAPTER 6

SECOND AND THIRD-GRADE LITERACY MAPS

ASSESSMENT AND TEACHING ACTIVITIES

Children who have met the first-grade benchmarks enter second grade as readers, writers, and spellers. They read and comprehend chapter books in which the text rather than pictures carry the burden of the content. Reading and writing are already construed to be meaningful, purposeful activities of choice. They already recognize over one hundred words automatically on sight and have a foundation of knowledge of basic regular phonics patterns. They spell many words correctly—up to two thirds of the words in their writing. They already have a beginning repertoire of good literature—both fiction and nonfiction—and have extensive knowledge about certain topics. They can already write with clarity and voice on topics about which they are passionate.

Third-grade learners do all of the above but at higher levels of sophistication. The chapter books they read and enjoy may have few, if any, pictures, though some books they enjoy have pictures for aesthetic enhancement. Their sight word recognition is beyond levels where it is reasonable to track it by counting the number of words they can recognize. They have mastered the basic high frequency, regular phonics patterns. They spell many words correctly and generally misspell fewer than 10% of the words they use in their writing. They make sophisticated text-to-self, text-to-text, and text-to-world knowledge connections. Reading and writing is, by choice, an established part of their lives.

USING THE SECOND AND THIRD-GRADE BENCHMARK CHECKLIST

The literacy maps for second and third grades address many of the same essential literacy requirements that have been discussed in detail in Chapters 4 and 5, but at higher levels of sophistication. Second and third graders must meet end-of-year benchmarks in Listening Comprehension, Exposure to Print, Reading Comprehension and Fluency, Word Specific Knowledge, Writing, Spelling, Ideas and World Knowledge, and Attitudes About Reading and Writing. There are some benchmark differences. By the time children enter second grade, they have fully mastered basic phonemic awareness, and children entering third grade have fully mastered basic regular phonics knowledge. Of course, even as literate adults, we continue to increase our phonemic awareness. Have you ever discovered a word that you had been pronouncing incorrectly? As an adult you increase your knowledge of phonics when you learn that the beginning /t/ sound of the word *phthisis (*pronounced tī sis) corresponds to the letters *phth*. The basic phonemic awareness and knowledge of regular phonics patterns is already mastered, however, before second and third grade, respectively.

ASSESSMENT AND TEACHING ACTIVITIES

How are your second or third graders progressing with literacy? The benchmark checklists on pages 140-150 and the guidelines in this chapter will help you answer this question about the development of each child in these critical years of literacy development. Here are the essential literacy elements you will address in second and third grades:

Second Grade

Listening Comprehension
Exposure to Print
Reading Comprehension
    and Fluency
Knowledge of Regular Phonics
    Patterns
Word Specific Knowledge
Writing
Spelling
Ideas and World Knowledge
Attitudes about Reading
    and Writing

Third Grade

Listening Comprehension
Exposure to Print
Reading Comprehension
    and Fluency
Word Specific Knowledge
Writing
Spelling
Ideas and World Knowledge
Attitudes about Reading
    and Writing

This chapter provides assessment tips and ways to receive feedback for each of the essential literacy requirements above, as well as teaching activities to help children meet benchmarks in the essential areas. As in kindergarten and first grade, benchmark assessment should start in September. Refer to pages 65-69 for a review of **Step One** and **Step Two** of the assessment process.

Here is a model for **Step One** using writing samples from second and third grades, respectively. Note that the writing samples may provide soft evidence rather than hard evidence that a benchmark is met or sometimes met. Soft evidence is valuable information, nevertheless, and this evidence can easily be corroborated by further observation in the classroom. For example, one good measure that a child is using sophisticated strategies in his or her reading is that you can see these same strategies being applied when the child writes.

A SECOND-GRADE WRITING SAMPLE TO MODEL STEP ONE

Read the sample of Blake's early second-grade writing presented in Figure 6.1.

Figure 6.1

If the sample in Figure 6.1 were selected for **Step One** of the September Baseline Benchmark Check, a baseline could be set for 22 of the 34 second-grade benchmarks.

ASSESSMENT OF 22 BENCHMARKS USING BLAKE'S WRITING

Benchmark 2-7. Blake's decision to write an expository piece is a pretty good indication that he reads and comprehends nonfiction. I would give him a ranking of "sometimes" on Benchmark 2-7.

Benchmark 2-8. The content of "Dive Into a Book" is evidence that Blake predicts and justifies. We would observe his reading to make sure he satisfied Benchmark 2-8 completely, but at minimum he already meets this benchmark "sometimes."

Benchmark 2-9. "Dive Into a Book" is full of "how," "who," and "what if" propositions. Blake's own writing indicates that he "sometimes" discusses "how," "who," and "what if" questions in nonfiction texts.

Benchmark 2-12. Blake read "Dive Into a Book" and accurately decoded regular, two-syllable words such as *little, mother, story,* and the three syllable word *every,* an indication that he meets Benchmark 2-4 at least some of the time.

Benchmark 2-13. Blake probably doesn't meet Benchmark 2-13. If he used knowledge of regular phonics patterns, he would decode *libore* as (li' boar) instead of *library.*

Benchmark 2-14. While only a rough indication, his reading and correct spelling of *know, people, brain, might, school, your,* and *cool,* indicate some higher level sight word recognition. He miscues on *quiet.* I would judge that he can recognize at least some second-grade-level words on sight.

Benchmark 2-15. Blake spells some second-grade-level words correctly in this piece as indicated in 2-14 above, but he misspells *I, father, hear, try,* and *little.* Although he spells some second grade level words correctly, he needs to learn many more, so he has only partly satisfied Benchmark 2-15.

Benchmark 2-16. This piece shows that Blake can read and spell some irregularly spelled words, for example, *know, people,* and *your,* indicating a baseline of "some words" but not "many second-grade words" for Benchmark 2-16 on accuracy in reading irregularly spelled words.

Benchmark 2-17. Blake's production demonstrated a good variety of longer compositions.

Benchmark 2-18. He is beginning to use formal language patterns such as beginning this piece with a rhetorical question.

Benchmark 2-19. The original version of "Dive Into a Book" was not revised or edited. Blake failed to correct even first-grade-level capitalization errors such as beginning each sentence with a capital letter, and first-grade level spelling errors such as *i* for *I*. His inconsistent spelling of *little*—spelled correctly twice but also spelled LITTE—goes unedited. He hasn't met Benchmark 2-19.

Benchmark 2-20. The evidence presented in 2-19 above shows Blake is not attending to spelling, mechanics, and presentation for final products.

Benchmark 2-21. Blake's Stage 4 spelling of most of the invented spelling in "Dive Into a Book" evidenced in spellings such as QUIET for *quit*, HERE for *hear*, TRAI for *try*, WAICH for *watch*, and STORYS for *stories*, demonstrates his spelling of many unknown words "by eye." He has met Benchmark 2-21.

Benchmark 2-22. He uses about one-third invented spelling in "Dive Into a Book."

Benchmark 2-23. He sometimes but not always spells common structural patterns and inflectional endings correctly. Note *helps, books, reading, can't, don't,* but also *STORYS.*

Benchmark 2-24. Previously studied second-grade-level words were spelled correctly in this story.

Benchmark 2-25. Blake expresses ideas, thinks creatively, and organizes information in ways that are appropriate for second grade.

Benchmark 2-26. Blake demonstrates age appropriate world knowledge and vocabulary.

Benchmark 2-28. Blake chooses to write independently.

Benchmark 2-30. Blake writes in a sustained way for a period of time.

Benchmark 2-32. Blake chooses writing related activities as enjoyment.

Benchmark 2-34. Blake chooses to write fiction and nonfiction in a variety of short compositions.

Now let's look at a sample of Blake's writing a year and several months later (Figure 6.2) and see what third-grade-level benchmarks may be assessed. (This piece was actually a letter I received written near the end of Blake's third-grade year, so it might have been used in the May Benchmark Check.)

Dear Uncle Richard,

I caught a carp that was three feet long and weighed eleven pounds. I was fishing at Urel's pond. I was fishing with bread. The fish were biting good all day but no sign of the carp. I was getting furious that the carp were not biting. I had been catching 12 to 13 inch bream around the dock. Then I decided to go all around the pond but I still didn't see or catch any carp. I got back to the dock and loaded the hook with bread. I threw out three large pieces of bread that were too large for the smaller fish to eat. Then I went to Urel's to get another half a loaf of bread. When I got back to the pond, one large piece of bread was gone and the ducks were at the other end of the pond. I noticed there were no small fish biting at the bread. Then I saw the large circles in the water—the biggest circles that I had seen all day. So I threw my bread out beside the dock pole where I saw the circles. Suddenly I saw my cork go speeding to the bottom. I reeled the fish in. It was a carp, finally! But right at the bank he got off. So I made a large bread ball and threw it out 15 yards ahead of the dock. I was about to stop fishing when the cork went under the water. I reeled the fish in, got the carp up to the dock, and got him in. He was pretty and VERY large. You are the only person who knows that I caught him from the dock.

The farm is doing good. Dad sold some cows and they brought a good amount of money—more than usual. Stacy says that it is cold up in old Boone and she says that she likes the second semester. Grandma is getting out a lot more than she was at Christmas.

p.s. Write me back.
Love, Blake

Figure 6.2

If the letter in Figure 6.2 were selected for **Step One** of the May Baseline Benchmark Check, 26 of the 40 third-grade benchmarks could be assessed.

ASSESSMENT OF 26 BENCHMARKS USING BLAKE'S LETTER

Benchmark 3-6. The sophistication of Blake's writing provides some soft evidence that he is likely to read and comprehend text appropriately designed for third grade. The best writers are likely to be good readers and Blake is decidedly a good third-grade writer. A "sometimes" rating for Benchmark 3-6 could be corroborated by observing Blake's reading of fiction and nonfiction.

Benchmark 3-7. Blake's ability to predict and justify—clearly evident in his fishing tale—likely echoes his use of this skill as a reader. I would mark Benchmark 3-7 "sometimes" and corroborate this finding by observing his reading.

Benchmark 3-8. Use of "how," "who," and "what if," questions are apparent in the fish story and might further be corroborated in Blake's reading.

Benchmark 3-11. The evidence that Blake incorporates cause and effect at a rather sophisticated level in writing—a skill he has likely gleaned as a reader—provides evidence of Benchmark 3-11. Additional evidence might be gathered from observing Blake read.

Benchmark 3-14. There is soft evidence in Blake's letter that his sight word recognition is developing nicely. He writes and correctly spells *bream, furious, weighed, threw, reeled,* and *pieces*—sophisticated words for a third-grade speller.

Benchmark 3-15. As cited in 3-14 above, Blake correctly spells a large collection of third-grade-level words.

Benchmark 3-16. Blake's letter indicates that he reads, writes, and spells irregular third-grade-level words accurately. Note *bream* (rhymes with *brim*), *pieces,* and *Boone.*

Benchmark 3-17. He uses prefixes and suffixes with accuracy in his writing. This is soft but not hard evidence to support some inference of word meaning from taught roots, prefixes, and suffixes. More observation of his reading would be necessary to verify Blake's progress with Benchmark 3-17.

Benchmark 3-18. Blake produces a good variety of compositions appropriate for grade three.

Benchmark 3-19. He uses formal language patterns and sophisticated vocabulary.

Benchmark 3-20. He went through the stages of the writing process.

Benchmark 3-21. He attended to spelling but needs additional support with paragraphing and use of the abbreviation *P.S.*

Benchmark 3-22. He "sometimes" uses a variety of formal sentence structures.

Benchmark 3-24. He reviews work for spelling but not always for mechanics with age-adequate success.

Benchmark 3-25. He sometimes makes use of elements of story structure. More writing observation would be needed to make a definitive judgment on Benchmark 3-25.

Benchmark 3-26. Blake is becoming a solid speller. He used the computer spell check on this piece and spelled all words correctly including the homophones *reel, bream, bread,* and *threw,* distinguishing them from *real, brim, bred,* and *through.*

Benchmark 3-27. Virtually accurate spelling is evident.

Benchmark 3-28. Common structural patterns and inflectional endings are spelled correctly.

Benchmark 3-29. Previously studied third-grade words are spelled correctly.

Benchmark 3-30. Blake used the computer spell check to correct unknown spellings in writing.

Benchmark 3-31. Blake's letter is one indication that he expresses ideas, thinks creatively, and organizes information in ways appropriate for third grade.

Benchmark 3-32. He has demonstrated age-appropriate world knowledge and vocabulary.

Benchmark 3-34. He chooses to write independently.

Benchmark 3-36. He chooses to write in a sustained way for a period of time.

Benchmark 3-38. He chooses to write for enjoyment—his letter is a good example of writing by choice.

Benchmark 3-40. He chooses to write fiction and nonfiction. (Interview finding.)

Identical procedures are followed in second and third grades for following **Step Two** as were presented for kindergarten and first grade. Here's a review of procedures for **Step Two:**

STEP TWO: Go through each remaining benchmark and consider each of the essential literacy requirements. Much of the assessment of the child's progress on the remaining benchmarks can be done observationally and in the context of daily classroom activity. (Next we will look at strategies and activities to help you assess and teach the essential literacy requirements of second and third grades.)

ASSESSMENT OVERVIEW

The basic principles for assessment are the same for second and third grades as were presented in detail for first grade beginning on page 65. Remember these basic principles: 1) You need a two-hour language arts block for successful teaching and literacy assessment. 2) You need to match each child to books that he or she can read.

The schedule presented in Chapter 3 on page 25 shows you how to organize the time children spend in a second and third-grade classroom. What changes at higher grade levels, of course, is the level of text children read and the level of sophistication of the content of instruction surrounding these text. In the following section, I model a book talk to demonstrate appropriate comprehension instruction for second and third grade and provide specific tips for making text-to-self, text-to-text, and text-to world knowledge connections. As you will see, the lesson is very different from a typical first-grade lesson. You will also see a shift in the word specific knowledge and spelling instruction as presented in a 15 minute per day spelling workshop which is described in detail beginning on page 120. In second and third grades, the type and timing of instruction shifts to allow more focus on higher level thinking skills. Compare the Comprehension and Fluency, and/or the Writing benchmarks at different grade levels. This will guide you in adjusting what may be construed as first, second, or third-grade-level instruction.

Having matched second and third graders with text that they can read and comprehend with accuracy, you set up a classroom where the expectation is 45 minutes of independent reading each day in school and 20 minutes of reading at home. Exposure to print and great reading volume become the expectation and bring gains in every essential literacy element area.

ASSESS LISTENING COMPREHENSION

A reading/writing second or third-grade class provides daily opportunities for the teacher to observe and interview individuals to assess listening comprehension. Assess after read-alouds, storytelling or during individual conferences. Provide practice for retelling and responding to material read aloud. See the suggestions made for grade one on page 69.

Here is a teaching activity to model sophisticated listening strategies needed by second and third graders—making text-to-self, text-to-text, and text-to-world knowledge connections. These are the same strategies your readers will use to improve reading comprehension.

TEACHING ACTIVITY: Modeling How Readers Think—Connecting Text-to-World Knowledge and Personal Experience

Schema theory (Maria, 1990) provides three ways to enhance comprehension by activating "mental files" before and during reading: 1) text-to-self connections, 2) text-to-text connections, and 3) text-to-world connections (Keene and Zimmermann, 1997). Modeling these connections shows children how to improve comprehension by relating unfamiliar text to their

own world knowledge and personal experience. Teachers can explicitly teach children to recall or activate schema or background knowledge.

The following vignette is a hypothetical read-and-think-aloud that I might conduct in a third-grade reading workshop. In this demonstration, I condense all three connecting forms (text-to-self, text-to-text, and text-to-world) into one lesson for demonstration purposes. In classroom practice, the teacher would model each of the connections separately in a variety of texts over a sustained period of time.

Gentry: Today in reading workshop, I will model how good readers think as they read in ways that will help their comprehension. First, I'll read a book to you by an author with whom I had dinner. Her name is Gloria Jean Pinkney. The book is entitled *Back Home.* Doesn't it have beautiful illustrations?

Gentry displays the book.

Gentry: Here's something interesting. *Back Home* was illustrated by the author's husband who is an award-winning artist. His name is Jerry Pinkney.

After we enjoy the story together, I'll read parts of *Back Home* again, but the second time, I'll stop and "think aloud" to show you what I was thinking when I read this book for the first time. Watch me stop, look up, and think aloud. Listen as I tell you about experiences I've had or things I know that are like the book in some way. Good readers do that, you know, they connect what they know and have experienced to what they read.

Today's story is about eight-year-old Ernestine who lives in a city "up North." She goes to Lumberton, North Carolina on a train to visit the place where her mother grew up, "back home." Here's the story, *Back Home,* by Gloria Jean Pinkney.

Gentry reads Back Home *in his native North Carolina accent. Then he reads the first page again and stops in the second paragraph after reading the following line .*

Text: He (Uncle June Avery) was waiting on the platform as the Silver Star slowly pulled into Robeson County Depot.

Gentry: "Wow, did I ever have a powerful thought after I read that line! You know, it just so happens my very own mama was born in Robeson County, North Carolina. Here's another coincidence. I rode that very same train, the Silver Star, when I was a little boy. It was my first train ride, and I have a very vivid memory of that experience. We left from the Robeson County Depot. What a coincidence I thought as I read this line—to find a book written about something I had experienced! This was the first time in many years that I had thought about my own first train ride. As I read this section, I could see myself in my mind—a little boy—getting onto a train that looked exactly like the one in the illustration. Since I could connect the text to myself and my own experience, I could imagine better how Ernestine in the story must have looked when she first saw her Uncle June waiting on the platform. I was making a text-to-self connection. Let's make a sign to help us remember that this is a good thinking process for proficient readers.

Gentry writes: Text-to-self: When you read something, let it bring back memories of something in your own life.

Gentry: This is a strategy good readers use. By remembering my own experience, I could understand the story better.

Gentry reads the next five pages stopping to think aloud and make text-to-self connections at various points in the text. At one point, Gentry stops and shifts mental gears.

Gentry: This book reminds me of another book I read, *Angela's Ashes* by Frank McCourt. It's an adult book but the author tells a story from his own childhood just like Gloria Pinkney did in *Back Home*. I thought of *Angela's Ashes* because I know that Gloria Pinkney wrote her story based on some of the events in her childhood. The authors have approached their life stories differently. Frank McCourt told his story exactly as it happened. Some people said he was too honest. He told some family secrets. Gloria took a different approach and actually created fiction by changing some of the characters and events from those in her real life. As I read this section, it popped into my mind how differently these authors chose to tell the stories from their childhood.

When readers remember another book as they read, they are making a text-to-text connection. Often a text-to-text connection is made when a character in a story reminds you of a character you read about in another story. In this case, my text-to-text connection was contrasting how two writers chose very different ways to tell their childhood stories.

Try to be a good reader and make text-to-text connections often. It not only increases understanding of what you read, but it helps you understand at a deeper level what you read. Let's make a sign to remind us to practice and talk about our text-to-text connections.

Gentry writes: Text-to-text: When you read something, let it remind you of another book or character you've read about. Make text-to-text connections like this:

_____ reminds me of _____

(the text you are reading)   (another text)

When Gentry reads the following line, he stops and looks up and there is a long pause before he speaks.

Text: "'Good night!' Ernestine said. She found Mama's old scrapbook in the bookcase and looked through it. I wish that old train didn't cost so much, she thought. Then Mama and Daddy could have come, too."

Gentry: You know what? This line really shocked me. The first time I read the story I remember thinking, "Wow, the author really is changing *Back Home* from what happened in her real life." Remember I told you that I actually met Mrs. Pinkney. She told me a lot about why she wrote this book and how things happened in her real life. I actually had a good bit of knowledge about Mrs. Pinkney before I read the book. That's sometimes called "world knowledge." I knew more about this book than most readers because I had the opportunity to meet the author. When you know a lot about something you are reading, you have "world knowledge," and it changes how you think when you read the book. Usually it helps you to understand better. Good readers try to make a connection with what they already know and the new things that they read. It's a good strategy. World knowledge helps you better understand what you read.

Sometimes, if you don't have enough background knowledge, you can't understand what you are reading. Then you have to learn more about the topic to help you understand the reading. Let's make a sign to help us remember this comprehension strategy.

Gentry writes: Text-to-world: Try to connect what you already know to new reading. Use your background knowledge. If you don't have enough background knowledge, learn what you need to know to help you understand.

Gentry ended the mini lesson by showing the class an inscription Gloria Jean Pinkney wrote to him when she autographed his copy of Back Home. *"The past is a key to our future works." The children discussed why they thought she decided to give him that special message.*

THINGS TO NOTE ABOUT MODELING TEXT-TO-SELF, TEXT-TO-TEXT, AND TEXT-TO-WORLD CONNECTIONS
(Adapted from Mosaic of Thought *by Keene and Zimmermann, 1997*)

- Demonstrate how good readers think by thinking aloud.
- Model text-to-self, text-to-text, text-to-world connections separately.
- Use a variety of books.
- Model over a sustained period of time.
- Make connections to other books.
- Generate lists of background knowledge on book topics.
- Identify concepts or themes to deepen comprehension before selecting the best texts to model.
- Think about where to pause and "think aloud" before modeling.
- Demonstrate how to use what is known about the author or the author's style to increase comprehension.
- Demonstrate how to read different kinds of text structure (e.g., nonfiction is often read more slowly and with more rereading than fiction).
- Demonstrate how to learn what is needed before reading when background knowledge is inadequate for understanding.
- Conduct short (10 or 15 minute) mini-lessons modeling with different books for a sustained period of time (e.g., text-to-text connections for a couple of weeks).
- Make it clear how your thinking helps you understand the text better.
- Initially keep illustrations clear and concise.
- Model first—delay inviting children to participate until they understand the concept being modeled.
- Invite children to share after a few demonstrations.
- During individual conferences, have children think aloud in their independent reading.
- Make classroom charts of text-to-text connections:
  Start with a book being read.
  List the title of a text with which it connects.
  Have children initial their contributions.

ASSESS EXPOSURE TO PRINT

Perhaps the most important job of the second and third-grade teacher, in addition to modeling higher level comprehension strategies and motivating children to read, is to match children with books or guide second and third graders to choose books that are just right for their higher reading levels. Follow the guidelines on page 75, Figure 5.2, for matching second and third graders to books.

Here are samples of texts to show you the level of sophistication of text that second and third graders, respectively, are expected to read and comprehend by the end of the year.

SAMPLES OF END OF YEAR, SECOND-GRADE TEXT

The Gooey Chewy Contest by Howard Goldsmith
(Matches Fountas and Pinnell criteria for Level N.)

Gabi laughed. Then everyone else started to laugh when they saw Gabi, still working his jaw up and down.

The judge signaled for Gabi to begin. Gabi took one last look at the smudged instructions, crossed his fingers, and put the gum in his mouth. After chewing it thoroughly, he began to blow.

A bubble the size of a golf ball slowly appeared. In no time it was as big as a baseball. Then something strange happened. To Gabi's amazement, the bubble began to blow itself! It swelled to the size of a basketball.

"Wow!" cried Pepita.

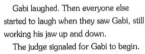

24

Everyone stared at the biggest bubble in the world. They waited for it to burst. But it continued to grow. It became twice as big as a basketball. Then three times as big!

How big would it get?

27

SAMPLES OF END OF YEAR, THIRD-GRADE TEXT

The BFG by Roald Dahl

(Level O, *Guided Reading*, Fountas and Pinnell, 1996)

Journey to London

The great yellow wasteland lay dim and milky in the moonlight as the Big Friendly Giant went galloping across it.

Sophie, still wearing only her nightie, was reclining comfortably in a crevice of the BFG's right ear. She was actually in the outer rim of the ear, near the top, where the edge of the ear folds over, and this folding-over bit made a sort of roof for her and gave her wonderful protection against the rushing wind. What is more, she was lying on skin that was soft and warm and almost velvety. Nobody, she told herself, had ever travelled in greater comfort.

Sophie peeped over the rim of the ear and watched the desolate landscape of Giant Country go whizzing by. They were certainly moving fast. The BFG went bouncing off the ground as though there were rockets in his toes

133

and each stride he took lifted him about a hundred feet into the air. But he had not yet gone into that whizzing top gear of his, when the ground became blurred by speed and the wind howled and his feet didn't seem to be touching anything but air. That would come later.

Sophie had not slept for a long time. She was very tired. She was also warm and comfortable. She dozed off.

She didn't know how long she slept, but when she woke up again and looked out over the edge of the ear, the landscape had changed completely. They were in a green country now, with mountains and forests. It was still dark but the moon was shining as brightly as ever.

Suddenly and without slowing his pace, the BFG turned his head sharply to the left. For the first time during the entire journey he spoke a few words. 'Look quick-quick over there,' he said, pointing his long trumpet.

Sophie looked in the direction he was pointing. Through the murky darkness all she saw at first was a great cloud of dust about three hundred yards away.

'Those is the other giants all galloping back home after their guzzle,' the BFG said.

Then Sophie saw them. In the light of the moon, she saw all nine of those monstrous half-naked brutes thundering across the landscape together. They were galloping in a pack, their necks craned forward, their arms bent at the elbows, and worst of all, their stomachs bulging. The strides they took were incredible. Their speed was unbelievable. Their feet pounded and thundered on the ground and left a great sheet of dust behind them. But in ten seconds they were gone.

134

'A lot of little girlsies and boysies is no longer sleeping in their beds tonight,' the BFG said.

Sophie felt quite ill.

But this grim encounter made her more than ever determined to go through with her mission.

It must have been about an hour or so later that the BFG began to slow his pace. 'We is in England now,' he said suddenly.

Dark though it was, Sophie could see that they were in a country of green fields with neat hedges in between the fields. There were hills with trees all over them and occasionally there were roads with the lights of cars

135

ASSESS READING COMPREHENSION

Consult the guidelines on pages 76-78 for Assess Reading Comprehension. In second and third grades, of course, you use these strategies with more sophisticated text that match the child's growing, independent reading level. Gradually, running records are replaced by book talks like the one modeled on pages 112-114. Expect second-grade- level readers to grow in reading sophistication to a point where they have the basic cueing system down pat. At that time you discontinue running records and your primary considerations for assessment and teaching reading comprehension and fluency become issues such as these:

SECOND GRADE

- Does the child have favorite authors and series and recognize similarities across books by one author or books in a series?
- Does the reader sometimes use knowledge of text structure when reading familiar genres, such as folk tales, reports, or instructions to enhance comprehension?
- Does the reader use features of the book, such as organization, contents, chapter headings, indexes, and glossaries, to assist reading for different purposes?
- Does the reader comment and answer questions to indicate that reading is interpretive and not just literal?
- Does the reader relate to characters in stories?

THIRD GRADE

- Does the reader change strategies depending on purpose for reading, such as skimming the overall text or scanning for specific information?
- Does the reader take different stances when reading fiction, such as being the observer and visualizing the scene, events, and characters, or being the character and feeling the character's emotions?
- Does the reader become critically aware of the intent or bias of the author and how the author can influence the reader?
- Is the reader able to follow diagrams in nonfiction, such as explanations, instructions, and reports and is he/she aware of the importance of integrating the illustrative material with the main text when reading nonfiction?

(Adapted from "Reading Assessment Checklist," *BookShop Literacy Program,* New York: Mondo Publishing, 1997)

Each child is assessed daily in the context of roving conferences during independent, guided, and shared reading. You are constantly observing, assessing, teaching, and motivating individual readers as well as the whole class of readers.

ASSESS WRITING

Earlier in the chapter, I modeled assessment of second and third-grade writing samples. Here's additional information to help you assess writing:

SECOND GRADE

- Does the writer have knowledge of punctuation for dialogue, and is he/she learning about using commas, and extending knowledge of using exclamation marks, and question marks?
- Can the writer research a topic and present information in an organized way?
- Can the writer demonstrate differences between fiction and nonfiction?
- Does the writer write in a variety of genres?

THIRD GRADE

- Is the writer more able to choose an appropriate genre to suit purpose and audience?
- Is the writer more likely to be consistent with time, place, and characters in a piece of writing?
- Is the writer able to think more about the best ways to present nonfiction using diagrams and labels rather than only large chunks of text?
- Is the writer becoming aware of the writing structures for some familiar genres, such as instructions and folk tales?

(From "Writing Assessment Checklist," *BookShop Literacy Program,* New York: Mondo Publishing, 1997)

ASSESS KNOWLEDGE OF REGULAR PHONICS PATTERNS

Second-grade teachers do assess children's knowledge of regular phonics patterns. Third graders who have mastered second-grade benchmarks enter third grade having mastered the basic core knowledge of regular phonics patterns. This is extended in third-grade spelling instruction where specific phonics instruction may take place in the context of spelling instruction. In general, however, basic phonics instruction drops out of the third grade curriculum.

In second grade, children are taught to look for syllable units and practice decoding polysyllabic words. Students accurately decode phonetically-regular, two-syllable words and two-syllable pseudowords (such as *cosnuv* and *uncabe*). By the end of second grade, knowledge of common letter-sound correspondences for two and three-syllable words enables skilled readers to read polysyllabic words effortlessly (Shefelbine, 1995, p. 4).

Remember, high frequency regular patterns should be mastered in first-grade. Many of the rarely occurring patterns are taught in second and third-grade spelling lessons. Samples of these words are provided under Assess Spelling on page 125. You must assess and be accountable for each individual's knowledge of regular phonics patterns. Second and third graders who haven't mastered first-grade phonics need individual intervention.

ASSESS WORD SPECIFIC KNOWLEDGE

By the end of second and third grade, children who meet the end-of-year benchmarks recognize so many words that it doesn't make a lot of sense to try to count the words as a measure of assessment. I recommend traditional, informal sight word assessment procedures, such as those used in the word recognition tests of informal reading inventories. If, from observing a child read second or third-grade-level texts, you suspect sight word recognition to be a problem, you can gain quick confirmation by using informal reading inventories. (See pages 160-161 for an informal reading inventory word recognition test.)

Assessment and teaching of word specific knowledge for second and third graders occurs with second and third grade spelling instruction. The following pages of this chapter show you how to conduct a spelling workshop, one of the best vehicles for both assessing and teaching second and third-grade-level, word specific knowledge.

ASSESS SPELLING

Getting Ready for Spelling Workshop Establish the routine of having each child keep a list of "Words I Need to Know How To Spell"—a personal word journal organized alphabetically. Keeping the list serves to make children conscious of looking for spelling words in their own writing and builds better spelling habits. Both the teacher and the student find words for the personal spelling word journal. The journal is also an assessment piece—a collection of words the child misspelled in writing, words that will eventually be studied during the year, words checked off after mastery, and words recycled which were studied and later found misspelled in writing.

TEACHING ACTIVITY: GREEN-PENNING WORDS

Help children find words they misspell in their writing by green-penning words. Here's how it works. Keep a green ink pen with you at all times. If you spot a developmentally appropriate, high-frequency word misspelled in a student's writing, circle the word, and write it correctly in green at the bottom of the page. Look for these words in anything the child writes. When the child sees a word you have written in green, it means "put this word in your spelling word journal." Green-pen two pages of each child's writing at least once every three weeks. Green-penning is for spelling only. Editing is a separate process.

(Adapted from J. Richard Gentry, September, 1997. "Spelling Strategies" *Instructor*. New York: Scholastic. p. 77)

TEACHING ACTIVITY: STUDENT-FOUND SPELLING WORDS

Students should also be responsible for finding misspelled words in their writing for their spelling journals. Once a week, have them follow these student-directed steps:

1. Circle three words on your draft that may be misspelled.
2. "Have a go" at spelling the words again. Try one of these:
   Visualize the word.
   Spell it like it sounds.
   Spell it by analogy to a spelling you know.
3. Find the correct spelling by asking someone, looking it up, or using a computer spell-checker.
4. Add the correctly spelled words to your list of "Words I Need To Know How to Spell."

(Adapted from J. Richard Gentry, September, 1997. "Spelling Strategies" *Instructor*. New York: Scholastic. p. 77)

Spelling Workshop: Monday (a 15-minute pretest) Each week, choose six developmentally appropriate words in second grade and 10 words in higher grades for a Monday pretest. Words may fit a pattern or spelling principle that is "the big idea" to be studied all week in the workshop. Follow these steps:

1. Call out each word, use it in a sentence, and call out the word again. Have students write the word.
2. Once all six (or 10) words have been written, write each word on the chalkboard.
3. Use "circle-dot" to assist students in correcting their own pretest.

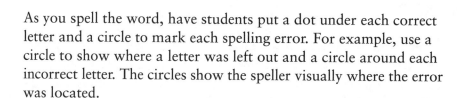

As you spell the word, have students put a dot under each correct letter and a circle to mark each spelling error. For example, use a circle to show where a letter was left out and a circle around each incorrect letter. The circles show the speller visually where the error was located.

Note the following important functions of the Monday pretest:

- *Assessing Spelling Levels.* Having tested students each Monday for four consecutive weeks with grade-appropriate words, you will have a good indication of their instructional level in spelling. Students who consistently spell 80% or 90% of the grade-level words correctly are above grade level spellers. Students who miss about half of the words, spell approximately on grade-level. Students who miss more than half are below grade-level spellers. (Henderson, 1990)
- *Finding Words.* Have second graders choose up to three words (five words for third graders) they misspell to write on their individual list for the week. Up to half of the words for their weekly individualized spelling list may come from the Monday Spell Check. Other words come from misspelled words in their writing and are collected in spelling journals.

Spelling Workshop: Tuesday (15 minutes for children to construct their weekly list) Have students create their word list on a sheet of paper with two columns labeled *School* and *Home*. Second graders make a six-word list; third graders make a 10-word list.

Traditionally, teachers are accustomed to 12 to 15 words per week at second-grade level and 20 words per week at third grade-level. What many teachers and parents don't realize is that traditional texts are designed so that second-grade-level spellers can already spell half of the words in the typical second-grade spelling list and third-grade-level spellers can already spell half of the words in a 20-word, third-grade spelling list (Henderson, 1990). This being the case, the typical third-grade student only learns 10 unknown words from a traditional 20-word list.

In the workshop model presented here, the shorter word list is economical and efficient. It's easier for children to manage a shorter list. Additionally, the words being studied are always words the student couldn't spell, words that were misspelled on the Monday Spell Check, or misspelled in writing.

Figure 6.3 presents typical individualized spelling lists for second and third-grade writers.

Second-Grader's List	Third-Grader's List
Misspelled on Monday Spell Check	**Misspelled on Monday Spell Check**
1. making	1. bare
2. doing	2. pear
3. riding	3. pair
	4. fare
Misspelled in Writing	5. fair
(from personal spelling journal)	
4. where	**Misspelled in Writing**
5. they	**(from personal spelling journal)**
6. house	6. pretty
	7. people
	8. scent
	9. scratch
	10. branches

Figure 6.3

If all words were spelled correctly on the Monday Spell Check, the entire list would come from the child's spelling journal.

Spelling Workshop: Wednesday/Thursday (15 minutes for children to practice and learn their weekly list) Children use various strategies to learn their individual words for the week. They may work independently or with partners. Good strategies include multimodal strategies such as the flip folder shown on page 124.

Sometimes children exchange lists and use game boards. The object is to spell a word correctly and be allowed to move forward. Partner work is engaging. It makes spelling study fun and eliminates busy work. Additionally, spelling partners are exposed to other children's words as they practice and learn their own.

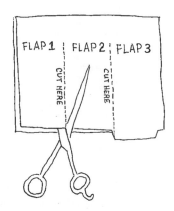

3. Flip Folder.

Flip folder is a variation of Ernest Horn's tried-and-true technique in use as far back as 1919. Here's an updated version of the famous look-say-cover-write-check technique with instructions for your child:

Make two cuts on the front of a standard manila folder to create three flaps.

FLAP 1   FLAP 2   FLAP 3

CUT HERE   CUT HERE

Write words to be studied in a column on a separate sheet of paper. Insert the sheet into the flip folder hiding the words to be studied under Flap 1.

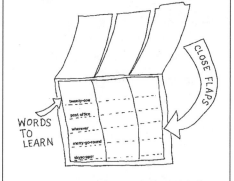

WORDS TO LEARN

CLOSE FLAPS

twenty-one
post office
wherever
merry-go-round
skyscraper

Now you are ready to look, say, see, write, and check.

Open Flap 1	**Look**	at the first word.
	Say	the first word.
Close all flaps	**See**	or visualize the word in your mind's eye
Open Flap 2	**Write**	the word in the center column.
Open Flaps 1 & 2	**Check**	your spelling.
Open Flap 3	**Rewrite**	the word in the third column from memory.

Spelling Workshop: Friday (15 minutes for Spell Check) Children exchange lists and test their partner. The teacher checks the quizzes as children finish. With the short 10-word list, it only takes a moment to check each list. Misspelled words are recycled in the personal spelling journal.

(Adapted from J. Richard Gentry, October, 1997, "Spelling Strategies" *Instructor.* New York: Scholastic. pp. 50-51)

Knowing the map for second and third-grade spelling includes an understanding of the kinds of spelling words and patterns to highlight in these important grades. Words chosen for spelling study should be the words and patterns children use in their writing. Here's a chart based on research to guide you in making good choices.

Second-Grade Spellers Should Be Mastering These Patterns:

Short vowel patterns in words like *sat, men, did, mom, cup, cash.*

Long vowel patterns in words like *made, nail, gray, sleep, clean, hide, dime, bright, might, dry, hope, nose, boat, show, cone.*

Consonant blends such as those made with S, L, and R in words like *stay, spot, black, glass, bring, frog.*

Plurals: *-s* and *-es* in words like *lips, eyes, birds, horses, classes.*

-ed and *-ing* endings in words like *wanted, played, rained, eating, making, doing, riding, running.*

Compound words such as *inside, baseball, raincoat, bluebird.*

Third-Grade Spellers Should Be Mastering These Patterns:

Plurals: *-s* and *-es* in words like *legs, bushes, cages, porches.*

Consonant blends in words like *scratch, scream, stretch, thread.*

Short vowels in words like *camp, clock, shock, kept, west.*

Long vowels in words like *paint, pony, own, bright, grew, rule.*

Combinations such as *-au-, -al-, -oi-,* in words like *taught, walking, oil.*

r-Controlled vowels in words like *hair, pear, cheer, fare.*

Contractions and compound words in words like *didn't, weren't, football, grandmother.*

Special spellings of sounds in words like *circle, pass, giant, join.*

Prefixes in words like *unhappy, preheat, unable, repaint.*

ASSESS IDEAS AND WORLD KNOWLEDGE AND ASSESS ATTITUDES ABOUT READING AND WRITING

Consult page 101 for explanations and teaching resources for Assess Ideas and World Knowledge and Attitudes about Reading and Writing.

In Chapter 6 we have looked at how to guide second and third graders on the journey to literacy. Earlier in *The Literacy Map,* we discussed the importance of knowing children individually, the importance of time, and the classroom schedule. Our discussion is not complete. I believe teaching is a craft that must be mastered. I also believe teaching is an art, and the art of teaching includes the purpose of seeking happiness. While problems may arise in the classroom, they are small in comparison to the happiness most teachers enjoy. In the next chapter, we consider "the joy of teaching."

CHAPTER 7

EXPERIENCE THE JOY OF TEACHING

Teaching should be joyful. On a flight to speak at a teacher's institute in San Diego, I sat next to a sophomore from Marquette University. An ROTC cadet dressed in summer whites, he had decided to major in secondary education. His vocation was growing out of the joy of teaching.

"Last year," he explained, "I had an opportunity to coach junior high school football. It was the most enjoyable experience of my life. I loved working with kids. Coaching football isn't really teaching..." He paused and changed his thought. "I *was* teaching them!" he exclaimed.

My niece had a similar experience. After her freshman year in college she took a summer job in a day camp. I called in July to wish her a happy nineteenth birthday.

"I love working with kids," she said, "especially eight-and nine-year-olds. *I'm going to major in elementary education.*"

The decision had come after she agonized for months about a major. She was inspired by the joy of teaching. Two years later, she was substitute teaching in a fifth grade classroom. One of the students said, "Miss Gentry, why are you always smiling?" (I think she was smiling because she was happy.) A little guy interjected, "She's smiling 'cause she's got the spirit!"

One of my goals in writing this book is to help you experience the joy of teaching. First and foremost, I hope it will help you meet the challenge of teaching literacy. For every kindergarten through third-grade teacher, that means understanding the literacy map and knowing each child individually.

Remember to establish clear goals. In meeting the literacy challenge, goals for each child must be very specific. I believe a problem with the recent nationwide focus on reading and language arts standards is that the standards lack much of the specificity necessary to be useful to teachers or to make sense to parents. Non-specific standards aren't very useful in helping teachers, parents, politicians, business leaders, or anyone else understand what children should know and be able to do at each grade level. Remember: *a curriculum that is not specifically defined cannot be instructionally supported.*

I believe this book will enable you to know whether you are successfully teaching what children who develop literacy must learn. The chapters provide clearly stated goals for each grade level with teaching strategies and assessment tools that enable you to provide instructional support, receive feedback, and monitor your own success in meeting the literacy challenge. The grade level literacy goals or benchmarks are tied to assessment so that you can know your students individually and check to see whether they are meeting grade specific benchmarks. Use these assessment tools to get the feedback you need.

Become absorbed in thinking about the literacy growth of each of your students. Talk about their literacy in the teacher's lounge, discuss them with your colleagues, and bring them home to the kitchen table. Think about each child's literacy growth every time you conference with a student, conduct a session of guided reading, or inspire an individual in a literature discussion group. You'll find helping a child achieve literacy is one of the greatest joys of teaching.

Once you focus your attention, have clear goals and receive appropriate feedback, your teaching will "flow" and your concentration will seem effortless. (Csilkszentmihali, 1990) This does not mean your teaching will be effortless. It means you will no longer *worry* about your efforts, instead, you will find enjoyment in the hard work of teaching. Nancie Atwell describes the complex relationship between joy and effort:

> These days I spend as much time on lesson planning and laying groundwork as I did back in the 1970s during my first years as a teacher. I am catching up—never relinquishing writing and reading workshop—but cultivating this garden by naming what I love as a reader and writer, researching what I don't know well enough to love, and imagining how to convey my love in the classroom. I am trying to be an adult writer and reader with such passionately held values that students will wish to apprentice themselves to me, trust they will learn from me, and love what they learn.
>
> This is hard, satisfying work. (Atwell, 1996, p. 16)

Teaching is hard, satisfying, joyful work. I hope *The Literacy Map: Guiding Children to Where They Need to Be* (K-3) enriched you with new skills and fresh achievement so that your own teaching challenges you to do your best, constantly improve your skills, and allow yourself to thoroughly enjoy your students and your classroom.

I believe you should be in complete control of your classroom. You should be the decision maker, because you are the one directly responsible for teaching your students. You are the one who can provide focused attention when and where it is needed to assure that each child progresses in literacy.

The paradox may be that you must be willing to give up the "safety" of "teacher-proof materials," legislated curricula, and mandated reading programs. *You* must ultimately be accountable in order to experience a feeling of control in your classroom. Your practices may be called into question and your professional judgments may be challenged by people outside your classroom—including those who are powerful but not well informed about the best teaching practices. But I believe you will be ready for these challenges.

Some educators are skeptical about specific, grade-level benchmarks. They fear teachers will lose control of their classrooms, that the curriculum will be dictated by the benchmarks. On the contrary, when debates in the public arena affect your life and daily work in your classroom, a good set of benchmarks is empowering. If you have clear goals and confidence in what you are doing, you don't need to fear that decisions about professional issues will be taken out of your hands. Your students' test scores *will* cut the mustard, and if they don't, you will have a satisfactory explanation because you know them as individuals, where they were functioning when they came to you, and where you have taken them.

One of my objectives has been to help you become better informed so that there is no mystery surrounding what to do about controversial literacy issues such as teaching phonemic awareness and phonics. If you understand phonemic awareness, phonics, spelling, the developmental integrity of benchmarks, and other aspects of literacy instruction, you can make wise instructional choices to deal with these aspects of literacy development without feeling threatened.

Assess and know your students individually. Be in control of your classroom and meet the literacy challenge for each child entrusted to your care. Reflect on what you are doing, why you do it, how you do it, and how well you do it. Do these things, and you will recognize when your teaching is "flowing." (Csilkszentmihali, 1990) You will experience the joy of teaching. You will "get the spirit."

BENCHMARK CHECKLISTS

The Benchmark Checklists on the following pages are provided for you to reproduce and place in the front of each child's portfolio as an individual assessment for that child.

Conduct ongoing benchmark checks for each child. I recommend formal benchmark checks in September, January, and May. These checks allow you to monitor each child as well as the effectiveness of your teaching.

- The purpose of the **September Baseline Benchmark Check** is to find out where each child is functioning at the start of the school year and to establish starting points of instruction.

- The **January Benchmark Check** is the midyear check to determine which benchmarks each child has achieved and those to strive for during the remaining months of the school year. The midyear check allows you to plan, teach, and assess more efficiently and effectively for the remainder of the year. Informal assessment should be ongoing in order to constantly inform your teaching.

- The **May Benchmark Check** allows you to be accountable for each child's literacy growth during the time he or she has been in your classroom. It allows you to trace each individual's growth and to record specific achievement in light of the goals you set in September.

Use the same checklist for September, January, and May, recording the dates beside your observation of whether a particular benchmark was "Not-Yet" met, "Some/Sometimes" met, or "All/Always" met. At the end of the year, you will not only verify that a child has reached a particular benchmark, but you will know where that child was at the beginning of the year with that benchmark, how progress toward reaching the benchmark developed, and when the benchmark was finally met.

Recommendations for how to assess the benchmarks are presented in Chapter 4 (for Kindergarten), Chapter 5 (for Grade One), and Chapter 6 (for Grades Two and Three).

KINDERGARTEN BENCHMARK CHECKLIST

NAME: _____

AGE: _____

TEACHER: _____

Record the date in the appropriate box for each question. Comment or give examples in the space provided.

LISTENING COMPREHENSION	Not Yet	Some/Sometimes	All/Always
K-1. Listens and comprehends stories read aloud			
K-2. Retells stories or parts of stories Comment or give examples: _____ _____ _____ _____ _____ _____			

EXPOSURE TO PRINT	Not Yet	Some/Sometimes	All/Always
K-3. Knows the parts of a book and their functions Check these: ____ front of book ____ cover ____ title ____ holds book correctly ____ turns pages left to right ____ relates pictures to content ____ points to print when reading or approximating reading ____ understands directionality			
K-4. Understands the concept of word (i.e., realizes that speech can be recorded in words; realizes what a printed word is)			
K-5. Makes the voice to print match when listening to familiar text read aloud			

READING COMPREHENSION	Not Yet	Some/Sometimes	All/Always
K-6. Uses own experiences and picture cues to help predict the meaning			
K-7. Realizes the message of the print is constant			
K-8. Approximates reading by looking at pictures in text and talking about the content of the text			

K-9. Becomes a novice reader. Reads a few pattern books and/or picture books from memory	Not Yet	Level A Books	Level B Books
Give some examples: _____ _____ _____ _____ _____ _____			

PHONEMIC AWARENESS	Not Yet	Some/Sometimes	All/Always
K-10. Understands that words are composed of speech sounds (e.g., *back* /b/ + /ak/)			
K-11. Identifies the constituent sounds in a one-syllable word (e.g., *play* /p/ + /l/ + /ā/)			
K-12. Identifies rhyming words			

KNOWLEDGE OF THE ALPHABET	Not Yet	Some/Sometimes	All/Always
K-13. Recites the letters of the alphabet			
K-14. Recognizes and names most of the uppercase and lowercase letters of the alphabet (Use the checklist on page 153.)			
K-15. Writes independently most of the uppercase and lowercase letters of the alphabet (Use the checklist on page 155.)			

BEGINNING PHONICS KNOWLEDGE	Not Yet	Some/Sometimes	All/Always
K-16. Understands the alphabet principle, that the sequence of letters in a written word represents the sequence of sounds (phonemes) in a spoken word			
K-17. Corresponds sound to the letters of the alphabet			

WORD SPECIFIC KNOWLEDGE	Not Yet	Some/Sometimes	All/Always
K-18. Recognizes some words by sight, including a few common words, names, and some environmental print (See the *Ohio Word Test* on page 156.)			

WRITING	Not Yet	Stage 1	Beyond Stage 1
K-19. Draws a picture that tells a story and approximates writing by labeling the picture or writing about the picture using Stage 1 spelling (Note: This is a midyear kindergarten benchmark.)			

	Not Yet	Stage 2	Beyond Stage 2
K-20. Draws a picture that tells a story and approximates writing by labeling the picture or writing about the picture using Stage 2 spelling (Note: This is an end of kindergarten year benchmark.)			
K-21. Uses the convention of leaving a space between words (Note: This is an end of kindergarten year benchmark.)			

SPELLING	Not Yet	Stage 1	Beyond Stage 1
K-22. Attempts to write or label using random letters for spelling (Note: This is Stage 1, Pre-communicative spelling. It is "the babbling level of spelling," and a midyear kindergarten benchmark.)			

	Not Yet	Stage 2	Beyond Stage 2
K-23. Spells words by matching some of the sounds in the words with an appropriate letter correspondence, such as KT for cat, BDA for birthday, or EKFH for egg (Note: This is Stage 2, Semiphonetic spelling. It is the "abbreviated spelling," and an end of kindergarten year benchmark.)			

SPELLING	Not Yet	Some/Sometimes	All/Always
K-24. Spells and writes his/her first name correctly			

IDEAS AND WORLD KNOWLEDGE	Not Yet	Some/Sometimes	All/Always
K-25. Expresses ideas, thinks creatively, and organizes information in ways that are appropriate for kindergarten Comment or give examples: _____ _____ _____ _____ _____			
K-26. Demonstrates age appropriate world knowledge Comment or give examples: _____ _____ _____ _____			

ATTITUDES ABOUT READING AND WRITING	Not Yet	Some/Sometimes	All/Always
K-27. Chooses reading related activities for enjoyment Comment or give examples: _____ _____ _____ _____ _____			
K-28. Chooses writing related activities for enjoyment Comment or give examples: _____ _____ _____ _____ _____			

FIRST-GRADE BENCHMARK CHECKLIST

NAME: _____

AGE: _____

TEACHER: _____

Record the date in the appropriate box for each question. Comment or give examples in the space provided.

LISTENING COMPREHENSION	Not Yet	Some/Sometimes	All/Always
1-1. Listens and comprehends appropriate content material designed for grade one			

EXPOSURE TO PRINT	Not Yet	Some/Sometimes	All/Always
1-2. Selects books at an appropriate text level			
1-3. Reads independently in a sustained way for a period of time			
1-4. Reads at home and at school			
1-5. Rereads books introduced in reading instruction or guided reading			

READING COMPREHENSION	Through Level D	Through Level G	Through Level I
1-6. Moves from novice, to practiced, to experienced reader.			
1-7. Reads aloud with fluency and comprehension any text that is appropriately designed for the first half of grade one			
1-8. Reads and comprehends both fiction and nonfiction text that is appropriately designed for the second half of grade one			

	Not Yet	Some/Sometimes	All/Always
1-9. Uses background knowledge to predict and justify what will happen next in stories appropriate for grade one			

READING COMPREHENSION	Not Yet	Some/Sometimes	All/Always
1-10. Discusses "how," "who," and "what if" questions in nonfiction texts appropriate for grade one			
1-11. Uses semantic, syntactic, and visual cues appropriately in first-grade-level text			

PHONEMIC AWARENESS	Not Yet	Some/Sometimes	All/Always
1-12. Demonstrates phonemic awareness by counting or clapping the number of syllables in a word			
1-13. Blends or segments phonemes in one syllable words			
1-14. Demonstrates full phonemic awareness (Note: Full phonemic awareness is a middle of first-grade benchmark.)			

KNOWLEDGE OF REGULAR PHONICS PATTERNS	Not Yet	Some/Sometimes	All/Always
1-15. Accurately decodes phonetically regular, one-syllable words (e.g., *web, milk, stamp, bake, boat*)			
1-16. Accurately decodes nonsense words such as *dit, nuv, buf, yode, shi, fler,* and *cleef* (Bryant, 1975)			
1-17. Uses phonics knowledge to sound out unknown words when reading text			

WORD SPECIFIC KNOWLEDGE	Not Yet	Some/Sometimes	Many
1-18. Recognizes common, irregularly spelled words by sight (e.g., *have, said, where, two*)			
1-19. Has a sight word vocabulary of 100 high frequency sight words	Not Yet	Some/Sometimes	100+
1-20. Spells a collection of first-grade-level words correctly (e.g., *the, at, bed, cut, five, green*)	Not Yet	Some/Sometimes	Many

WRITING	Not Yet	Some/Sometimes	Good Variety
1-21. Produces a variety of short compositions (e.g., stories, simple descriptions, journal entries)			

	Not Yet	Some/Sometimes	All/Always
1-22. Uses basic punctuation and capitalization			

SPELLING	Not Yet	Stage 3	Beyond Stage 3
1-23. Spells words by matching all of the sounds in the word with an appropriate letter correspondence, such as EGL for *eagle*, BOTM for *bottom*, or UNITD for *united* (Note: This is Stage 3, Phonetic spelling. It is "spelling by ear" and a midyear, first-grade benchmark.)			

	Not Yet	Stage 4	Beyond Stage 4
1-24. Spells words by representing many of the visual aspects of English spelling, such as e-marker pattern, double letters, vowels in all syllables, and vowel digraphs in spellings like EGUL for eagle, BOTUM for bottom, or YOUNIGHTED for united (Note: This is Stage 4, Transitional spelling. It is "spelling by eye," and an end of first-grade benchmark.)			

	Not Yet	Some/Sometimes	Many
1-25. Spells many three and four letter phonetically regular, short vowel words correctly (e.g., *bat, sit, milk*)			
1-26. Spells some high frequency, phonetically regular, long vowel words correctly (e.g., *like, take, day*)			
1-27. Spells some high frequency, irregular sight words correctly (e.g., *of, the, one,* and *have*)			

IDEAS AND WORLD KNOWLEDGE	Not Yet	Some/Sometimes	All/Always
1-28. Expresses ideas, thinks creatively, and organizes information in ways that are appropriate for grade one Comment or give examples:			

1-29. Demonstrates age appropriate world knowledge Comment or give examples:			

ATTITUDES ABOUT READING AND WRITING	Not Yet	Some/Sometimes	All/Always
1-30. Chooses to read independently Comment or give examples:			

1-31. Chooses to write independently Comment or give examples:			

ATTITUDES ABOUT READING AND WRITING	Not Yet	Some/Sometimes	All/Always
1-32. Chooses to read in a sustained way for a period of time Comment or give examples:			
1-33. Chooses to write in a sustained way for a period of time Comment or give examples:			
1-34. Chooses reading related activities for enjoyment Comment or give examples:			
1-35. Chooses writing related activities for enjoyment Comment or give examples:			

ATTITUDES ABOUT READING AND WRITING	Not Yet	Some/Sometimes	All/Always
1-36. Chooses to read both fiction and nonfiction Comment or give examples:			

_____

_____

_____

_____

	Not Yet	Some/Sometimes	All/Always
1-37. Chooses to write fiction and nonfiction in a variety of short compositions Comment or give examples:			

_____

_____

_____

_____

SECOND-GRADE BENCHMARK CHECKLIST

NAME: _____

AGE: _____

TEACHER: _____

Record the date in the appropriate box for each question. Comment or give examples in the space provided.

LISTENING COMPREHENSION	Not Yet	Some/Sometimes	All/Always
2-1. Listens and comprehends appropriate content material designed for grade two			

EXPOSURE TO PRINT	Not Yet	Some/Sometimes	All/Always
2-2. Reads extensively fostering listening comprehension, conceptual understandings, vocabulary, and world knowledge appropriate for grade two			
2-3. Reads longer chapter books with few illustrations by end of grade two			
2-4. Selects and reads trade books appropriate for grade two			

READING COMPREHENSION AND FLUENCY	Not Yet	Some/Sometimes	All/Always
2-5. Reads aloud with fluency and comprehension any text that is appropriately designed for the first half of grade two			
2-6. Uses phonics knowledge to sound out words, including multi-syllable words, when reading text			
2-7. Reads and comprehends both fiction and nonfiction text that is appropriately designed for the second half of grade two			
2-8. Uses background knowledge to predict and justify what will happen next in stories appropriate for grade two			

READING COMPREHENSION AND FLUENCY	Not Yet	Some/Sometimes	All/Always
2-9. Discusses "how," "who," and "what if" questions in nonfiction texts appropriate for grade two			
2-10. Reads nonfiction materials for answers to specific questions			
2-11. Increases sophistication in using semantic, syntactic, and visual cues appropriately in second-grade-level text			

PHONEMIC AWARENESS	Not Yet	Some/Sometimes	All/Always
• Fully Mastered			

KNOWLEDGE OF REGULAR PHONICS PATTERNS	Not Yet	Some/Sometimes	All/Always
2-12. Accurately decodes phonetically regular two syllable words			
2-13. Accurately decodes two syllable pseudo words, such as *cosnuv, uncabeness* (Bryant, 1975)			

WORD SPECIFIC KNOWLEDGE	Not Yet	Some/Sometimes	Many
2-14. Increases sight word recognition to include second-grade-level words			
2-15. Spells correctly a collection of second grade level spelling words and spelling patterns, such as diphthongs, special vowel spellings, and common word endings			
2-16. Accurately reads many irregularly spelled words			

WRITING	Not Yet	Some/Sometimes	Good Variety
2-17. Produces longer compositions (e.g., stories, descriptions, journal entries)			

	Not Yet	Some/Sometimes	All/Always
2-18. Begins to use formal language patterns in place of oral language patterns in writing			
2-19. Begins to use revision and editing processes to clarify and refine his/her own writing			

WRITING	Not Yet	Some/Sometimes	Good Variety
2-20. By the end of grade two, begins to attend to spelling, mechanics, and presentation for final products (Second graders should not be expected to correct all spelling independently.)			

SPELLING	Not Yet	Stage 4	Beyond Stage 4
2-21. Continues to spell many unknown words "by eye" (i.e., Stage 4, transitional spelling) while using specific word knowledge to spell an increasing number of second-grade-level words correctly			

	Not Yet	Some/Sometimes	All/Always
2-22. Moves from inventing about one third of the spellings in pieces of independent writing to more accurate spelling			

	Not Yet	Some/Sometimes	Mostly
2-23. Begins to spell common structural patterns and inflectional endings correctly			
2-24. Spells previously studied second grade level words and spelling patterns in his/her own writing			

IDEAS AND WORLD KNOWLEDGE	Not Yet	Some/Sometimes	All/Always
2-25. Expresses ideas, thinks creatively, and organizes information in ways that are appropriate for grade two Comment or give examples: _____ _____ _____ _____			
2-26. Demonstrates age appropriate world knowledge, expanding ideas and vocabulary Comment or give examples: _____ _____ _____ _____			

ATTITUDES ABOUT READING AND WRITING	Not Yet	Some/Sometimes	All/Always
2-27. Chooses to read independently			

Comment or give examples:

_____

_____

_____

_____

2-28. Chooses to write independently			

Comment or give examples:

_____

_____

_____

_____

2-29. Chooses to read in a sustained way for a period of time			

Comment or give examples:

_____

_____

_____

_____

2-30. Chooses to write in a sustained way for a period of time			

Comment or give examples:

_____

_____

_____

_____

ATTITUDES ABOUT READING AND WRITING	Not Yet	Some/Sometimes	All/Always
2-31. Chooses reading related activities for enjoyment Comment or give examples:			

_____

_____

_____

_____

| 2-32. Chooses writing related activities for enjoyment

Comment or give examples: | | | |

_____

_____

_____

_____

| 2-33. Chooses to read both fiction and nonfiction

Comment or give examples: | | | |

_____

_____

_____

_____

| 2-34. Chooses to write fiction and nonfiction in a variety of short compositions

Comment or give examples: | | | |

_____

_____

_____

_____

THIRD-GRADE BENCHMARK CHECKLIST

NAME: _____

AGE: _____

TEACHER: _____

Record the date in the appropriate box for each question. Comment or give examples in the space provided.

LISTENING COMPREHENSION	Not Yet	Some/Sometimes	All/Always
3-1. Listens and comprehends appropriate content material designed for grade three			

EXPOSURE TO PRINT	Not Yet	Some/Sometimes	All/Always
3-2. Reads extensively, fostering listening comprehension, conceptual understandings, vocabulary, and world knowledge appropriate for grade three			
3-3. Reads fairly lengthy chapter books appropriate for grade three			
3-4. Selects and reads trade books appropriate for grade three			

READING COMPREHENSION AND FLUENCY	Not Yet	Some/Sometimes	All/Always
3-5. Reads aloud with fluency and comprehension any text that is appropriately designed for the first half of grade three			
3-6. Reads and comprehends both fiction and nonfiction text that is appropriately designed for the second half of grade three			
3-7. Predicts and justifies what will happen next in stories appropriate for grade three			
3-8. Discusses "how," "who," and "what if" questions in nonfiction texts appropriate for grade three			

READING COMPREHENSION AND FLUENCY	Not Yet	Some/Sometimes	All/Always
3-9. Discusses similarities in characters and events across stories			
3-10. In interpreting fiction, discusses underlying theme or message			
3-11. In interpreting nonfiction, distinguishes cause and effect, fact and opinion, main idea and supporting details			
3-12. Uses multiple resources to locate information (e.g., table of contents, index, available technology)			
3-13. Increases sophistication in using semantic, syntactic, and visual cues as evidenced in reading third-grade-level text			
KNOWLEDGE OF REGULAR PHONICS PATTERNS	Not Yet	Some/Sometimes	All/Always
• Basic patterns are fully mastered.			
WORD SPECIFIC KNOWLEDGE	Not Yet	Some/Sometimes	Many
3-14. Increases sight word recognition to include third-grade-level words			
3-15. Spells correctly a collection of third-grade-level spelling words			
3-16. Extends accuracy in reading many irregularly spelled words			
3-17. Infers word meaning from taught roots, prefixes, and suffixes			
WRITING	Not Yet	Some/Sometimes	Good Variety
3-18. Produces longer compositions appropriate for grade three (e.g., stories, descriptions, journal entries)			

WRITING	Not Yet	Some/Sometimes	All/Always
3-19. Uses formal language patterns in his/her own writing, including literate syntax and larger vocabulary			
3-20. Uses prewriting, drafting, revision, and editing processes in producing compositions and reports			
3-21. Attends to spelling, mechanics, and presentation for final products (Third-grade-level spellers should be expected to correct most but not all spelling independently.)			
3-22. Uses a variety of formal sentence structures in his/her own writing			
3-23. Writes fairly sophisticated reports combining information from multiple sources			
3-24. Independently reviews work for spelling mechanics and presentation with age-adequate success			
3-25. Uses elements of story structure including setting, imaginative story lines, changing episodes, story grammar elements, and interesting vocabulary with age-adequate success			

SPELLING	Not Yet	Stage 4	Beyond Stage 4
3-26. Continues to spell many unknown words "by eye" (i.e., Stage 4, transitional spelling) while using specific word knowledge to spell an increasing number of third-grade-level words correctly			

3-27. Invents less than ten percent of spellings in pieces of independent writing	Not Yet	Some/Sometimes	Mostly

3-28. Spells most common structural patterns and inflectional endings correctly by end of grade three			

SPELLING	Not Yet	Some/Sometimes	All/Always
3-29. Spells previously studied third grade level words and spelling patterns in his/her own writing			
3-30. Uses the dictionary and other resources to check and correct unknown spellings in writing			

IDEAS AND WORLD KNOWLEDGE	Not Yet	Some/Sometimes	All/Always
3-31. Expresses ideas, thinks creatively, and organizes information in ways that are appropriate for grade three Comment or give examples:			

_____

_____

_____

_____

	Not Yet	Some/Sometimes	All/Always
3-32. Demonstrates age appropriate world knowledge, expanding ideas and vocabulary Comment or give examples:			

_____

_____

_____

_____

ATTITUDES ABOUT READING AND WRITING	Not Yet	Some/Sometimes	All/Always
3-33. Chooses to read independently Comment or give examples:			

_____

_____

_____

_____

ATTITUDES ABOUT READING AND WRITING	Not Yet	Some/Sometimes	All/Always
3-34. Chooses to write independently Comment or give examples:			

_____

_____

_____

_____

| 3-35. Chooses to read in a sustained way for a period of time

Comment or give examples: | | | |

_____

_____

_____

_____

| 3-36. Choose to write in a sustained way for a period of time

Comment or give examples: | | | |

_____

_____

_____

_____

| 3-37. Chooses reading related activities for enjoyment

Comment or give examples: | | | |

_____

_____

_____

_____

ATTITUDES ABOUT READING AND WRITING	Not Yet	Some/Sometimes	All/Always
3-38. Choose writing related activities for enjoyment Comment or give examples:			
3-39. Chooses to read both fiction and nonfiction Comment or give examples:			
3-40. Chooses to write fiction and nonfiction in a variety of short compositions Comment or give examples:			

(A part of these benchmarks is an adaptation of Appendix A: Benchmarks or Grade-level Competencies. *Dallas Reading Plan.* Dallas: Dallas Independent School District, 1997. Other resources consulted include Washington State's *A Framework for Achieving the Essential Academic Learning Requirements in Reading* and North Carolina's *Comprehensive Reading Plan for North Carolina Public Schools, and Spelling through Phonics,* Marlene J. McCracken and Robert A. McCracken. 1985. Winnipeg. MB: Peguis Publishers Limited. Spelling stages are explicated in *My Kid Can't Spell* by J. Richard Gentry. 1997. Portsmouth, NH: Heinemann.)

RUNNING RECORD

Name:_____ Date_____

Analysis of Errors and Self Corrections

	M Meaning
	S Structure
Easy ☐ Instructional ☐ Challenging ☐	V Visual

Page #		# of Errors	# of SC	Information Used	
				Error Analysis	Self Correction Analysis
	Title/Text:_____ Text Reading Level_____ Seen Text_____ Unseen Text_____			M S V	M S V

Adapted from Marie Clay. *The Early Detection of Reading Difficulties* (Heinemann).

RUNNING RECORD SCORING FORM

Count all the words in the book or passage excluding the title. This gives the running words. Subtract the number of errors from the total number of running words. Divide the remainder by the number of running words. Multiply by 100 to get a percentage.

$$\frac{\text{Running words - Errors}}{\text{Running words}} \times 100 = \underline{\hspace{1.5cm}}\%$$

Independent   95% or above
Instructional   90-94%
Too hard   89% or below

Appropriate Strategies Observed

___ Reads with fluency
___ Uses picture cues
___ Reads for meaning
___ Sounds it out
___ Uses visual clues
___ Uses syntactic cues
___ Uses semantic cues
___ Self-corrects
___ Makes appropriate guesses

Disruptive Strategies Observed

___ Not fluent
___ Ignores pictures
___ Doesn't make sense
___ Doesn't use phonics
___ Ignores visual clues
___ Ignores syntax
___ Ignores semantics
___ Doesn't self-correct
___ Guesses too much

Comprehension
Prompt a retelling or ask comprehension questions.

Prompts for retelling:
How did the story begin? What happened next?
What happened in the story?
Tell me the story in your own words.
What is this story about?

___ excellent   ___ fairly good   ___ fragmentary   ___ illogical

Adapted from Marie Clay. *The Early Detection of Reading Difficulties* (Heinemann).

ALPHABET CHECKLIST
(Letter Recognition)

Name: _____

Age: _____

Teacher: _____

As the child names the letters, circle the letters not known.

A	B	C	D	E	F
G	H	I	J	K	L
M	N	O	P	Q	R
S	T	U	V	W	X
Y	Z				

a	b	c	d	e	f
g	h	i	j	k	l
m	n	o	p	q	r
s	t	u	v	w	x
y	z				

ALPHABET CHECKLIST
(Random Order)

Name: _____

Age: _____

Teacher: _____

As the child names the letters, circle the letters not known.

e	h	l	w	s	p
i	r	a	t	y	d
b	g	q	c	j	f
k	n	u	z	m	x
v	o				

E	H	L	W	S	P
I	R	A	T	Y	D
B	G	Q	C	J	F
K	N	U	Z	M	X
V	O				

ALPHABET CHECKLIST
(Writing)

Name: _____

Age: _____

Teacher: _____

Aa	Bb	Cc	Dd
Ee	Ff	Gg	Hh
Ii	Jj	Kk	Ll
Mm	Nn	Oo	Pp
Qq	Rr	Ss	Tt
Uu	Vv	Ww	Xx
Yy	Zz		

OHIO WORD TEST—ADMINISTRATION SHEET

Ask a child to read one list. Help child with the practice word, if necessary: do not score it. Do not help with other words and do not use the list for teaching. Use alternative lists for retesting.

LIST A	LIST B	LIST C
PRACTICE WORD can	PRACTICE WORD in	PRACTICE WORD see
and	ran	big
the	it	to
pretty	said	ride
has	her	him
down	find	for
where	we	you
after	they	this
let	live	may
here	away	in
am	are	at
there	no	with
over	put	some
little	look	make
did	do	eat
what	who	an
them	then	walk
one	play	red
like	again	now
could	give	from
yes	saw	have

From Marie M. Clay. *An Observation Survey*, Appendix 1 (Heinemann).

OHIO WORD TEST SCORE SHEET

TEST SCORE

/20

Date: _____

Name: _____

School: _____

Recorder: _____ Classroom Teacher: _____

Record incorrect responses.
Choose appropriate list of words. ✓ (Checkmark) Correct Response • (Dot) No Response

LIST A	LIST B	LIST C
PRACTICE WORD	PRACTICE WORD	PRACTICE WORD
can	in	see
and	ran	big
the	it	to
pretty	said	ride
has	her	him
down	find	for
where	we	you
after	they	this
let	live	may
here	away	in
am	are	at
there	no	with
over	put	some
little	look	make
did	do	eat
what	who	an
them	then	walk
one	play	red
like	again	now
could	give	from
yes	saw	have

From Marie M. Clay. *An Observation Survey*, Appendix 1 (Heinemann).

COMMON IRREGULARLY SPELLED WORDS CHECKLIST
(Reading Sight Word Recognition)

Child's Name: _____

Teacher's Name: _____

Date of Assessment: _____

Assessment Codes
N= Not Yet   S= Sometimes   A= Almost Always

	ASSESSMENT CODE	COMMENTS		ASSESSMENT CODE	COMMENTS
to			know		
was			two		
have			world		
on			where		
here			before		
were			live		
there			buy		
are			through		
said			read		
one			bear		
some			clothes		
own			hour		
too			what		
our					

THE GENTRY DEVELOPMENTAL SPELLING TEST SCORING SHEET
For Two Administrations

STAGE

STAGE

1. _____ _____

2. _____ _____

3. _____ _____

4. _____ _____

5. _____ _____

6. _____ _____

7. _____ _____

8. _____ _____

9. _____ _____

10. _____ _____

Name: _____

Date: _____

Stage: _____

1. _____ _____

2. _____ _____

3. _____ _____

4. _____ _____

5. _____ _____

6. _____ _____

7. _____ _____

8. _____ _____

9. _____ _____

10. _____ _____

Name: _____

Date: _____

Stage: _____

INFORMAL READING INVENTORY
(Word Recognition Test: Grades 1-2)

Child's Name: _____   Teacher's Name: _____

Date of Assessment: _____

	Sight	Analysis		Sight	Analysis
(Grade 1)			**(Grade 2)**		
1. little*	_____	_____	1. feel	_____	_____
2. next*	_____	_____	2. drink	_____	_____
3. reads	_____	_____	3. wave	_____	_____
4. my*	_____	_____	4. gray	_____	_____
5. make*	_____	_____	5. start*	_____	_____
6. old*	_____	_____	6. horn	_____	_____
7. mother	_____	_____	7. across*	_____	_____
8. bed	_____	_____	8. warm*	_____	_____
9. grow*	_____	_____	9. bad	_____	_____
10. laugh	_____	_____	10. even*	_____	_____
11. near*	_____	_____	11. feed	_____	_____
12. before*	_____	_____	12. always*	_____	_____
13. lamb	_____	_____	13. round*	_____	_____
14. ride	_____	_____	14. country	_____	_____
15. store	_____	_____	15. enough*	_____	_____
16. high*	_____	_____	16. able	_____	_____
17. began*	_____	_____	17. should*	_____	_____
18. made*	_____	_____	18. bottom	_____	_____
19. cry	_____	_____	19. crawl	_____	_____
20. her*	_____	_____	20. machine	_____	_____

*denotes basic sight word from Revised Dolch List

Number Correct _____   _____   Number Correct _____   _____

Total_____   Total _____

Scoring Guide for Graded Word Lists

Independent	Instructional	Frustration
20 19	18 17 16 15 14	13 or less

From **Basic Reading Inventory** by Jerry L. Johns. Kendall/Hunt Publishing Company

INFORMAL READING INVENTORY
(Word Recognition Test: Grades 3-4)

Child's Name: _____ Teacher's Name: _____

Date of Assessment: _____

	Sight	Analysis		Sight	Analysis
(Grade 3)			**(Grade 4)**		
1. star	_____	_____	1. bike	_____	_____
2. net	_____	_____	2. castle	_____	_____
3. doctor	_____	_____	3. jungle	_____	_____
4. spoon	_____	_____	4. bullet	_____	_____
5. trap	_____	_____	5. factory	_____	_____
6. valley	_____	_____	6. stripe	_____	_____
7. shirt	_____	_____	7. problem	_____	_____
8. meet	_____	_____	8. target	_____	_____
9. chuckle	_____	_____	9. capture	_____	_____
10. gaze	_____	_____	10. sleeve	_____	_____
11. rib	_____	_____	11. pump	_____	_____
12. discover	_____	_____	12. sausage	_____	_____
13. hundred	_____	_____	13. electric	_____	_____
14. reason	_____	_____	14. business	_____	_____
15. conductor	_____	_____	15. instant	_____	_____
16. coast	_____	_____	16. balance	_____	_____
17. escape	_____	_____	17. surround	_____	_____
18. thirty	_____	_____	18. invention	_____	_____
19. prepare	_____	_____	19. accident	_____	_____
20. nation	_____	_____	20. rifle	_____	_____

Number Correct _____ _____   Number Correct _____ _____

Total_____   Total _____

Scoring Guide for Graded Word Lists

Independent	Instructional	Frustration
20 19	18 17 16 15 14	13 or less

From **Basic Reading Inventory** by Jerry L. Johns. Kendall/Hunt Publishing Company

BOOK LIST K-3

(LEVELS A-P)

LEVEL A
Kindergarten/Grade One

Title	Author	Publisher
The Applebird	Wildsmith, Brian	Oxford
At the Zoo	Kloes, Carol	Kaeden Books
Colours	Pienkowski, Jan	Penguin
Count and See	Hoban, Tana	Penguin
I Paint	Madian, Jon	Mondo
Look What I Can Do	Aruego, José	Macmillan
My Book	Maris, Ron	Viking
My Class	Stewart, J. and Salem, L.	Seedling
One Hunter	Hutchins, Pat	Greenwillow
Play Ball	Vandine, JoAnn	Mondo

LEVEL B
Kindergarten/Grade One

Barney's Horse	Hoff, Syd	Harper Trophy
Cat on the Mat	Wildsmith, Brian	Oxford
Colors in the City	Urmston, K. and Evans, K.	Kaeden Books
Fun With Hats	Malka, Lucy	Mondo
Here's Skipper	Salem, L. and Stewart. J.	Seedling
Honk!	Smith, Sue	Mondo
I Get Tired	Stewart, J. and Salem, L.	Seedling
Marching Band	Urmston, K. and Evans, K.	Kaelen Books
Mommy, Where Are You?	Ziefert, Harriet and Boon, Emile	Puffin Books
Who Lives in the Sea?	James, Sylvia M.	Mondo

LEVEL C
Grade One

Title	Author	Publisher
Brown Bear, Brown Bear	Martin, Bill	Holt
Cool Off	Diaz, Nellie	Mondo
I Love Bugs	Lake, Mary Dixon	Mondo
In the City	Pasternac, Susana	Scholastic
My Dream	Wildsmith, Brian	Oxford
Now We Can Go	Jonas, Ann	Greenwillow
Playhouse for Monster	Mueller, Virginia	Whitman
Rain	Kalan, Robert	Greenwillow
Roll Over!	Peck, Merle	Clarion
Spots, Feathers and Curly Tails	Tafuri, Nancy	Morrow

LEVEL D
Grade One

Title	Author	Publisher
At the Beach	Hunt, R. and Brychta, A.	Oxford
The Ball Bounced	Tafuri, Nancy	Morrow
The Chick and Duckling	Ginsburg, Mirra	Macmillan
How Many Bugs in a Box?	Ginsburg, Mirra	Macmillan
Is This a Monster?	Lovell, Scarlett and Snowball, Diane	Mondo
It Didn't Frighten Me	Goss, Janet L. and Harste, Jerome C.	Mondo
Monster Can't Sleep	Mueller, Virginia	Puffin Books
Noisy Breakfast	Blonder, Ellen	Scholastic
Oops!	Mayer, Mercer	Penguin
School Bus	Crews, Donald	Morrow

LEVEL E
Grade One

Title	Author	Publisher
Days of Adventure	Swanson-Natsues, Lyn	Mondo
Foot Book	Seuss, Dr.	Random House
Go Dog Go	Eastman, P.D.	Random House
Herman the Helper	Kraus, Robert	Simon & Schuster
Inside, Outside, Upside Down	Berenstain, Stan and Jan	Random House
It Looked Like Spilt Milk	Shaw, Charles	Harper & Row
Oh No!	Scarfee, Bronwen	Mondo
The Rummage Sale	Hunt, R. and Brychta, A.	Oxford
Where Can It Be?	Jonas, Ann	Morrow
Where's Spot?	Hill, Eric	Putnam

LEVEL F
Grade One

Title	Author	Publisher
Across the Stream	Ginsburg, Mirra	Morrow
Amy Loves the Sun	Hoban, Julia	Scholastic
Cat Goes Fiddle-i-fee	Rockwell, Anne	Dutton
A Cat in the Tree	Galdone, Paul	Houghton Mifflin
Just Like Daddy	Asch, Frank	Simon & Schuster
Marmalade's Nap	Wheeler, Cindy	Knopf
Peter's Painting	Moss, Sally	Mondo
Pip at the Zoo	Oxford Reading Time	Oxford
Rosie's Walk	Hutchins, Pat	Macmillan
Tarantulas Are Spiders	Platnick, Norman	Mondo

LEVEL G
Grade One

Title	Author	Publisher
Alligator Shoes	Dorros, Arthur	Dutton
Angus Thought He Was Big	Hoban, Julia	Scholastic
A Bedtime Story	Fox, Mem	Mondo
Chickens	Snowball, Diane	Mondo
The Dog	Barton, Byron	HarperCollins
Jason's Bus Ride	Ziefert, Harriet	Penguin
Lydia and Her Kitten	Rayner, Shoo	Oxford
More Spaghetti I Say	Gelman, Rita	Scholastic
Over in the Meadow	Shulevitz, Uri	Scribner
Ten Sleepy Sheep	Keller, Holly	Morrow

LEVEL H
Grade One

Title	Author	Publisher
The Awful Mess	Rockwell, Anne	Four Winds
Come Out and Play Little Mouse	Kraus, Robert	Morrow
George Shrinks	Joyce, William	HarperCollins
If I Had an Alligator	Mayer, Mercer	Dial
My Brown Bear Barney	Butler, Dorothy	Morrow
Put Me in the Zoo	Lopshire, Robert	Random House
Seven Little Monsters	Sendak, Maurice	HarperCollins
We Are Best Friends	Aliki	Morrow
What's Cooking?	Harwayne, Shelley	Mondo
When the King Rides By	Mahy, Margaret	Mondo

LEVEL I
Grade One (late)

Title	Author	Publisher
Albert the Albatross	Hoff, Syd	HarperCollins
Alligators All Around	Sendak, Maurice	HarperCollins
Angus the Cat	Flack, Marjorie	Viking
Are You My Mother?	Eastman, P.D.	Random House
The Dancing Dragon	Vaughan, Marcia	Mondo
Fix-It	McPhail, David	Penguin
Floating and Sinking	Andersen, Honey	Mondo
Hattie and the Fox	Fox, Mem	Bradbury
Noisy Nora	Wells, Rosemary	Scholastic
The Very Busy Spider	Carle, Eric	Philomel

LEVEL J
Grade Two (early)

Title	Author	Publisher
Charlie Needs a Cloak	dePaola, Tomie	Prentice-Hall
Green Eggs and Ham	Seuss, Dr.	Random House
Henry and Mudge	Rylant, Cynthia	Aladdin
Jamberry	Degen, Bruce	Harper & Row
Little Blue and Little Yellow	Lionni, Leo	Scholastic
The Snowy Day	Keats, Ezra Jack	Scholastic
Somewhere	Baskwill, Jane	Mondo
Some Machines Are Enormous	Bird, Bettina and Short, Joan	Mondo
The Very Hungry Caterpillar	Carle, Eric	Putnam
Where the Wild Things Are	Sendak, Maurice	Harper & Row

LEVEL K
Grade Two

Title	Author	Publisher
Arthur's Honey Bear	Hoban, Lillian	HarperCollins
Bear Goes to Town	Browne, Anthony	Doubleday
Bony-Legs	Cole, Joanna	Scholastic
Frog and Toad Together	Lobel, Arnold	HarperCollins
The Greedy Goat	Bolton, Faye (retold by)	Mondo
It Takes a Village	Cowen-Fletcher, J.	Scholastic
Madeline	Bemelmans, L.	Scholastic
Nate the Great and the Lost List	Sharmat, Marjorie Weinman	Bantam Doubleday Dell
Sheila Rae, the Brave	Henkes, Kevin	Scholastic
The Story of Hungbu and Nolba	T' ae-hyon, Kang (retold by)	Mondo

LEVEL L
Grade Two

Title	Author	Publisher
Animal Tracks	Dorros, Arthur	Scholastic
Cam Jansen and the Mystery Of Flight 54	Adler, David A.	Puffin Books
Edgar Badger's Balloon Day	Kulling, Monica	Mondo
George and Martha	Marshall, James	Houghton Mifflin
Make Way for Ducklings	McCloskey, Robert	Puffin Books
Pinky and Rex	Howe, James	Avon Books
The Secret at the Polk Street School	Reilly Giff, Patricia	Bantam Doubleday Dell
Stories Julian Tells	Cameron, Ann	Random House
Thinking About Ants	Brenner, Barbara	Mondo
Through Grandpa's Eyes	MacLachlan, P.	Harper Trophy

LEVEL M
Grade Two

Title	Author	Publisher
Can Do, Jenny Archer	Conford, Ellen	Little Brown
A Chair for My Mother	Williams, Vera B.	Scholastic
The Chalk Box Kid	Bulla, Clyde Robert	Random House
Cloudy With a Chance Of Meatballs	Barrett, Judi	Atheneum
Freckle Juice	Blume, Judy	Dell Yearling
Frogs	Tyler, Michael	Mondo
Julian's Glorious Summer	Cameron, Ann	Random House
Molly's Pilgrim	Cohen, Barbara	Bantam Doubleday Dell
Monster for Hire	Wilson, Trevor	Mondo
Second Grade–Friends Again!	Cohen, Miriam	Scholastic

LEVEL N
Grade Three

Title	Author	Publisher
Amber Brown Is Not A Crayon	Danziger, Paula	Scholastic
The Enormous Crocodile	Dahl, Roald	Puffin Books
The Gooey Chewy Contest	Goldsmith, Howard	Mondo
Hannah	Whelan, Gloria	Random House
Horrible Harry and the Green Slime	Kline, Suzy	Puffin Books
Look at the Moon	Garelick, May	Mondo
Most Wonderful Doll In the World	McGinley, Phyllis	Scholastic
The Mystery of Pony Hollow	Hall, Lynn	Random House
No Room for a Dog	Kane Nichols, Joan	Avon Books
Shark in School	Giff, Patricia Reilly	Bantam Doubleday Dell

LEVEL O
Grade Three

Title	Author	Publisher
Adventures of Ali Baba Bernstein	Hurwitz, Johanna	Avon Books
Beezus and Ramona	Cleary, Beverly	Avon Books
Boxcar Children: Bicycle Mystery	Warner, Gertrude Chandler	Albert Whitman
Bunnicula	Howe, James	Avon Books
The Lucky Stone	Clifton, Lucille	Bantam Doubleday Dell
Make a Wish, Molly	Cohen, Barbara	Bantam Doubleday Dell
Mario's Mayan Journey	McCunney, Michelle	Mondo
Miss Geneva's Lantern	Lake, Mary Dixon	Mondo
Matilda	Dahl, Roald	Puffin Books
The Whipping Boy	Fleischman, Sid	Troll

LEVEL P
Grade Three

Title	Author	Publisher
Amelia Earhart	Parlin, John	Bantam Doubleday Dell
Baseball's Best, Five True Stories	Gutelle, Andrew	Random House
Baseball's Greatest Pitchers	Kramer, S. A.	Random House
Five Brave Explorers	Hudson, Wade	Scholastic
George's Marvelous Medicine	Dahl, Roald	Puffin Books
Helen Keller	Graff, Stewart and Polly Anne	Bantam Doubleday Dell
Jesse Owens: Olympic Hero	Sabin, Francene	Troll
One Day in the Tropical Rain Forest	George, Jean Craighead	Harper Trophy
A Pony Named Shawney	Small, Mary	Mondo
Sugar Cakes Cyril	Gershator, Phillis	Mondo

* The letters listed for the levels refer to the leveling identified in *Guided Reading* by Irene C. Fountas and Gay Su Pinnell.

REFERENCES

Allen, R.V. 1976. *Language Experiences in Communication.* Boston, MA: Houghton Mifflin.

Atwell, Nancie. 1996. "Cultivating Our Garden" *Voices From the Middle.* Urbana, IL: National Council of Teachers of English. (November. Vol. 3, No. 4).

Atwell, Nancie. 1998. *In the Middle.* Portsmouth, NH: Heinemann.

Bryant, N. D. 1975. *Diagnostic Test of Basic Decoding Skills.* New York: Columbia University, Teachers College.

Burmeister, L. 1975. *Words—From Print To Meaning.* Reading, MA: Addison-Wesley.

Calkins, Lucy with Shelley Harwayne. 1991. *Living Between the Lines.* Portsmouth, NH: Heinemann.

Calkins, Lucy. 1998. "Rethinking the Reading Workshop." Featured speaker for North Carolina Reading Association Conference. March 3, 1998. Winston-Salem, NC.

Calkins, Lucy. 1996. "Re-Imagining the Reading/Writing Workshop" a one-day seminar sponsored by Heinemann Workshops, April 19, 1996. Braintree, MA.

Carnine, Douglas. 1980. "Two Letter Discrimination Sequences: High-Confusion Alternatives First Versus Low-Confusion Alternatives First." *Journal of Reading Behavior,* 12 (1), 41-47.

Chall, Jeanne. 1967. *Learning to Read: The Great Debate.* New York: McGraw-Hill.

Chomsky, Carol, 1979. "Approaching Reading Through Invented Spelling," B. Resnick & P. A. Weaver (Eds), *Theory and Practice of Early Reading,* Volume 2. Erlbaum, Hillsdale, New Jersey, 179.

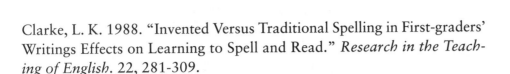

Clarke, L. K. 1988. "Invented Versus Traditional Spelling in First-graders' Writings Effects on Learning to Spell and Read." *Research in the Teaching of English.* 22, 281-309.

Clay, M. 1993. *The Early Detection of Reading Difficulties.* Portsmouth, NH: Heinemann.

Clay, M. 1993. *Reading Recovery: A Guidebook for Teachers in Training.* Portsmouth, NH: Heinemann.

Clay, M. 1993. *An Observation Survey of Early Literacy Achievement.* Portsmouth, NH: Heinemann.

Comprehensive Reading Plan for North Carolina's Public Schools. 1997. Raleigh, NC: Public Schools of North Carolina.

Crévola, Carmel A. and Peter W. Hill. 1998. "The Role of Standards in Educational Reform for the 21st Century" (Chap. 6) in *Preparing Our Schools for the 21st Century.* (David D. March, ed.) Alexandria, Virginia: Association for Supervision and Curriculum (p.129).

Crévola, Carmel A. and Peter W. Hill. 2000. *Class: Children's Literacy Success Strategy.* Mondo Publishing.

Csilkszentmihalyi, Mihaly. 1990. *Flow: The Psychology of Optimal Experience.* New York: HarperPerennial.

Cunningham, Pat. M., and Richard L. Allington. 1994. *Classrooms That Work: They Can All Read and Write.* New York: HarperCollins.

Cunningham, Pat M. 1995. *Phonics They Use: Words for Reading and Writing,* 2nd ed.; New York: Harper Collins College Publishers.

Dahl, Karin, and Patricia Scharer. 1998. Research report to Reading: Orthography and Word Perception Special Interest Group, May 16, 1998. International Reading Association 43rd Annual Convention, Orlando, Florida.

Dallas Reading Plan. 1997. "Appendix A: Benchmarks or Grade-level Competencies." Dallas, TX: Dallas Independent School District.

Damon, William, 1995. *Greater Expectations.* New York: The Free Press. p. 208.

Ehri, L. C. and L. S. Wilce. 1987. "Does Learning to Spell Help Beginners Learn to Read Words?" *Reading Research Quarterly.* 22, pp. 47-65.

Fiderer, Adele. 1995. *Practical Assessments for Literature Based Reading Classrooms.* New York: Scholastic, Inc.

Flesch, Rudolf. 1985. *Why Johnny Can't Read* (1955 renewed 1985) New York: Harper & Row, (p. 147).

Fountas, Irene C. and Gay Su Pinnell. 1996. *Guided Reading*. Portsmouth, NH: Heinemann.

Fountas, Irene C. and Gay Su Pinnell. 1999. *Matching Books to Readers*. Portsmouth, NH: Heinemann.

A Framework for Achieving the Essential Academic Learning Requirements in Reading. 1997. State of Washington: Superintendent of Public Instruction.

Glazer, Susan Mandel. 1992. *Reading Comprehension: Self-Monitoring Strategies to Develop Independent Readers*. New York: Scholastic.

Gentry, J. Richard. 1978. "An Analysis of Developmental Spelling In GNYS AT WRK." *The Reading Teacher*. 36 (2): 192-200.

Gentry, J. Richard. 1985. "You Can Analyze Developmental Spelling." *Teaching K-8*. 15 (9): 44-45.

Gentry, J. Richard. 1997. *My Kid Can't Spell!* Portsmouth, NH: Heinemann.

Gentry, J. Richard and Jean W. Gillet. 1993. *Teaching Kids To Spell*. Portsmouth, NH: Heinemann.

Gentry, J. Richard. 1997. "Spelling Strategies." *Instructor*. New York: Scholastic. September 1997, pp. 76-77.

Gentry, J. Richard. 1997. "Spelling Strategies." *Instructor*. New York: Scholastic. October 1997, pp. 50-51.

Goodman, Yetta, Dorothy Watson, and Carolyn Burke. 1987. *Reading Miscue Inventory: Alternative Procedures*. Katonah, NY: Richard C. Owen.

Goswami, Usha. 1996. *Rhyme and Analogy Teacher's Guide*. New York: Oxford University Press, p. 5.

Graves, Donald H. 1983. *Writing: Teachers and Children at Work*. Portsmouth, NH: Heinemann.

Graves, Donald H. 1994. *A Fresh Look at Writing*. 1994. Portsmouth, NH: Heinemann.

Henderson, Edmund. 1990. *Teaching Spelling*. Boston, MA: Houghton Mifflin.

Henry, Tamara, and Beth Ashley. 1997. "The Push is on to Ensure Literacy by Third Grade." *USA Today*. Cover story, Section D. January 29, 1997.

Hirsch, E. D. Jr. 1987. *Cultural Literacy: What Every American Needs to Know.* Boston, MA: Houghton Mifflin.

Hirsch, E. D. Jr. (Ed.). 1991. *What Your First Grader Needs To Know.* The Core Knowledge Series. New York: Delta.

Independent Reading Guide. 1997. Published by School District of Philadelphia, based on work by South Brunswick, New Jersey School District. Debbie Chagin, Elaine Culbertson, Dr. Eileen Feldgus, Carol Hirshfeld, Dr. Adrienne Jacoby, Ellen Johnson, Regina Katz, Dr. Susan Neuman, Donna Piekarski, Elizabeth Zack.

Johns, Jerry L. 1997. *Basic Reading Inventory: Preprimer Through Grade Twelve & Early Literacy Assessment.* Kendall/Hunt Publishing Company.

Juel, Connie. 1994. *Learning to Read and Write in One Elementary School.* New York: Springer-Verlag.

Juel, Connie. 1996. "Learning to Read and Write: A Longitudinal Study of Fifty-four Children from First Through Fourth Grade." *Journal of Educational Psychology,* 80, 437-447.

Keene, Ellin O. and Susan Zimmermann. 1997. *Mosaic of Thought.* Portsmouth, NH: Heinemann.

Maria, K. 1990. *Reading Comprehension Instruction: Issues and Strategies.* Timonium, MD: York Press.

McCracken, Marlene J. and Robert A. McCracken. 1985. *Spelling through Phonics.* Winnipeg, MB: Peguis Publishers Limited.

Read, Charles. 1975. *Children's Categorization of Speech Sounds in English.* Urbana, IL: National Council of Teachers of English.

"Reading Assessment Checklist" from *BookShop Literacy Program,* 1997. New York. Mondo Publishing.

Reading Today, "Reading Report Raises Hopes, "Volume 15, Number 5, April/May 1998, p. 4.

Richgels, Donald J. 1995. "Invented Spelling Ability and Printed Word Learning in Kindergarten." *Reading Research Quarterly.* Vol. 30, No. 1 (pp. 96-109).

Roper/Schneider, H. D. W. 1984. *Spelling, Word Recognition, and Phonemic Awareness Among first-grade Children.* Unpublished doctoral dissertation, University of Texas, Austin.

Routman, Regie. 1991, 1994. *Invitations*. Portsmouth, NH: Heinemann.

Routman, Regie. 1997. *Literacy at the Crossroads*. Portsmouth, NH: Heinemann.

Shanahan, Timothy. 1997. "Reading-Writing Relationships, Thematic Units, Inquiry Learning...In Pursuit of Effective Integrated Literacy Instruction." *The Reading Teacher* Vol. 51. No. 1 September 1997, p. 16.

Shefelbine, John. 1995. "Learning and Using Phonics in Beginning Reading." *Scholastic Literacy Research Paper*. New York: Scholastic. Vol. 10, p. 4.

Smith, C. B. and G. M. Ingersoll. 1984. *Written Vocabulary of Elementary School Pupils: Ages 6—14, pp. 33-42*. Bloomington, IN: Indiana University Monographs in Language and Reading Studies, No. 6.

Smith, Frank. 1994. *Understanding Reading: A Psycholinguistic Analysis of Reading and Learning to Read*. 5th ed. Hillsdale, NJ: Lawrene Erlbaum Associates, Publishers.

Snow, Catherine, E., Susan Burns, and Peg Griffin (Eds.) 1998. *Preventing Reading Difficulties in Young Children*. Washington, DC: National Academy Press.

Stanovich, Keith E. 1994. "Romance and Reality." *The Reading Teacher*. 47, pp. 280-291.

Taberski, Sharon. "Success in Reading: Guided Reading in Your Classroom," a one-day workshop sponsored by Mondo Publishing, Chicago, IL. April 22, 1997.

"Writing Assessment Checklist" from *BookShop Literacy Program*, 1997. New York. Mondo Publishing.

Wylie, Richard E. and Donald D. Durrell. "Teaching Vowels Through Phonograms." *Elementary English Journal*. Vol. 47, Oct 1970. pp. 787-791.